Practical Suggestions for Teaching

A. Harry Passow & Gary A. Griffin
Series Editors

The Value Realms:
Activities for Helping Students Develop Values

Practical Suggestions for Teaching

OTHER TITLES IN THE SERIES:

The Value Realms

ACTIVITIES FOR
HELPING STUDENTS DEVELOP VALUES

Vincent Presno
Wright State University
&
Carol Presno

Teachers College, Columbia University
New York & London   1980

Library of Congress Cataloging in Publication Data

Presno, Vincent
   The value realms.

 (Practical suggestions for teaching)
 Includes index.
 1. Moral education. 2. Values. I. Presno, Carol,
joint author. II. Title. III. Series.
LC268.P64   370.11'4   80-13051
ISBN 0-8077-2584-6 (pbk.)

Manufactured in the United States of America
7 6 5 4 3 2 1 80 81 82 83 84 85

CONTENTS

Part III
Activities Interrelating the Value Realms and Dimensions

FOREWORD

There is little doubt that each person, explicitly or implicitly, demonstrates value positions about the multiple phenomena in his or her immediate world as well as in the broader society. For most, this is a constant activity. Schools, as instruments of the culture, offer ideal places in which to observe these expressions of value. Teachers and students make choices from multiple options. Preferences are put forth and acknowledged. Likes and dislikes, sometimes in extreme forms, are central to the lives of schools. These instances, and many others, are issues of values and valuing.

A central question for teachers, given the persistence of value-laden judgments in classroom settings, is how to help students understand and develop their own value stances regarding the people, places, events, and ideas which surround them. It is unlikely that any human interaction can be (or should be) value free. The central purposes of this book are to acknowledge that valuing is a reality of human activity and to provide teachers with specific and concrete strategies for helping students understand and act upon this aspect of being human.

Vincent and Carol Presno have developed and tested more than eighty value activities for classroom use. These activities emerge from a well-grounded theoretical model and are presented in this book in clear and straightforward form for classroom action. The movement from theory to recommended practice is not easy. It requires disciplined thinking, flexibility of pedagogical orientation, and a precise understanding of the nature of classroom life. The Presnos have demonstrated a firm grasp of this enormously difficult planning activity. The underlying theory is carefully selected, the activities have been tested with many classroom teachers and students, and the pages which follow reflect the revisions which resulted from "real world" experience.

There have been times in educational circles when "value free teaching and learning" were considered not only reasonable but feasible. Experience has taught us that there is danger in this position. The danger emerges from a misunderstanding of the ways people express themselves through arts, technology, and human interactions. Young people who are not aware of the nature of value and how it influences their lives are at a major disadvantage in personal, social, emotional, political, and economic arenas. Although schools have recently attended to values, the attention has been less than systematic. This book provides teachers with classroom-tested ways to sharpen and deepen that attention.

In contrast to other curriculum materials with value orientations, the Presnos have developed activities which move beyond the general and into the specific areas of human activity about which we all develop and express values. Valuing is defined and presented in terms of the psychological, the social, the economic, the ethical, the social-ethical, the esthetic, the poetic and literary, the technological and scientific, and the legal. The similarities and differences between and among these are clearly noted and the activities which are presented are directly and logically linked to the specific value realm under discussion.

This book can be a major and important contribution to classroom life. As in all cases of suggestions for instruction, the true test will be the degree to which teachers and students find them useful and satisfying. The inital experiences of those who have used these materials suggest that attention to the value realms can be an enriching, rewarding, and meaningful addition to schools and the young people and adults in them.

GARY A. GRIFFIN
Director of the Division of Instruction
Teachers College, Columbia University

PREFACE

It is important that practical work in value education be based on sound value theory, just as good work in mathematics education must be based on a sound conception of number. Robert S. Hartman's theory of value presents a thoroughly rationalized conception and lends itself to precise and accurate application to curriculum and teaching. This work is based on Hartman's theory. The essentials of the theory as applied to curriculum and teaching are more fully analyzed in Vincent Presno's doctoral dissertation, "Strategies for Value Teaching" (Teachers College, Columbia University, 1975). This book is the direct practical application of some aspects of the theory; it presents a variety of teaching activities following a brief theoretical review of terms and concepts.

We have received much support and encouragement for this work. Professor Arno A. Bellack has constantly supported our efforts to apply Hartman's theory to curriculum and teaching. His sense for the "language of the classroom" has given needed direction for the transition from theory to practice. Professor Philip H. Phenix has from the beginning recognized the potential of Hartman's theory for application to value education. His interpretations and recommendations have helped to focus the work on the aspects of the theory that are significant for education. The book has benefited from the editorial skills of Professor Gary A. Griffin, whose early suggestions helped to give it form and direction.

Dr. Roger G. Iddings, Dean of the College of Education at Wright State University, has contributed to the progress of the project by establishing my work on it as a task priority and by providing needed time and facilities.

V.P.

PART I

Introduction

Chapter 1

A UNIFIED APPROACH TO VALUES

An important perspective is emergent in curriculum, instruction, and teaching. Educators are concerned about dealing with values. It is no longer considered adequate to present facts, explanations, and descriptions. Teachers are being asked to help students make ethical and moral decisions, to encourage students to become involved in the political life of their communities, to enhance students' awareness of esthetic values. Teachers are asked to help students function in social and community roles, make economic decisions such as career choices and consumer choices, and develop their own abilities and motivations.

This book presents activities that teachers may use to help students think about and make value judgements in a broad range of value realms. The particular value realms developed are ethical, social, social-ethical, esthetic, poetic and literary, psychological, economic, legal, and technological. Some of the activities are designed to help students interrelate these various value realms.

Various writers have defined and advocated many and varied types of values for curriculum and teaching. Raths, Harmin, and Simon stress the importance of personal choice and of prizing on the basis of *consequences*. Abraham Maslow focuses on *self-actualization* as the most significant value to be fostered in schools. The supporters of confluent education emphasize *affect*. Oliver and Shaver suggest that American cultural standards such as *dignity and freedom* are the kinds of values that need development in education. Lawrence Kohlberg concentrates on the ethical and moral values of

3

principled autonomy. For the followers of Counts and Butts, *citizenship and democratic processes* are values that must be central to teaching and curriculum.

Each of these approaches focuses on a particular kind of value—reflective prizing, self-actualization, affect, cultural standards, citizenship, principled autonomy. Each approach develops a limited view of value and tends to neglect the types of value stressed in the other approaches.

The approach applied in this book is based on a general and comprehensive concept of value developed by Robert S. Hartman. From a generic definition of value various subtypes of value are derived. The valuable in general (goodness in general) is defined in terms of conceptual fulfillment. Something is valuable (good) if it fulfills its conceptual properties. The value of citizenship, the value of the self-actualizing individual, the value of affective preference—these and other types of value are related to the idea of value-in-general. They are viewed as different types of conceptual fulfillment. This approach produces an integrated conception of value in which specific values have the good-in-general in common.

A DEFINITION OF VALUE

Whenever something is judged for its value, it is judged in terms of a concept of it. Whenever we value something, we are comparing the thing to the idea we have of it. For example, if my idea of a "car" is that it has an engine, doors, brakes, four wheels, a steering system, and so forth, I will compare a particular car to this idea. If the particular car is lacking its doors and one of its wheels, I will judge the car to have very little value. But if it has all or most of the qualities contained in my idea or concept of "car," then I decide it has considerable value. I might say, "It is a good car."

The most general definition of value, then, is that whenever a thing fulfills or matches or corresponds to our idea of it, then it has value. If it lacks some qualities of our idea, then to some extent it lacks value. Language has many terms that are used to express value or lack of it: *good, valuable, no good, bad, not valuable, worthless,* and so on.

Whenever a being thinks rationally, that is, combines concepts with objects, then he will have a term in his language connoting that a concept corresponds to an object and vice versa, and this is the term that in our languages is called "good," "bon," "gut," "jo," "khoroshii," etc.[1]

Something that has worth or value completely conforms to the full idea of that thing. When a person, group, or object is fully what it is, it has value. For example, "That is a good table" means not only that a certain piece of furniture *is* a table; but also that it is *fully* a table — a complete table. It has all the properties of the *idea* of "table."

Some instances of things *not* fully conforming to the full idea of that kind of thing: a "person in love" who does not feel tender, a "nurse on duty" who is asleep, a "peaceful country" that starts a war. Some instances of things being fully what they are: a person fully living his life, a kingly king, a comedian's comedian.

THE VALUE REALMS

Value is the fulfillment of concepts or ideas. Value may be applied to many fields of human activity. Specific value types — such as social value, ethical value, economic value — originate by applying the idea of value to different areas of life. Economic value is the fulfillment of economic concepts by things. Ethical value is the fulfillment of ethical concepts by persons. Psychological value is the fulfillment of psychological concepts by persons. Social value is the fulfillment of social concepts by groups. For example, an important social concept is role expectation; social value is persons fulfilling the idea of role expectation.

Ethical goodness is expressed by the terms *honest, sincere, authentic.* Psychological goodness is expressed in terms of *motivations, feelings, attitudes. Beauty* is esthetic goodness. *Expensive* denotes that which is economically valuable. Social-ethical goodness is *freedom, democracy.* That which is socially valuable is *duty* or *responsibility.* The poetic good is identified by terms such as *literary* and *metaphorical. Lawful, constitutional,*

---

[1]From *The Structure of Value: Foundations of Scientific Axiology* by Robert S. Hartman (p. 110). Copyright© 1967 by Southern Illinois University Press. Reprinted by permission of the Southern Illinois University Press.

just represent the legal good. Technological good is expressed by terms such as *engineered* and *operational*.

Each of the value realms is a specific type of goodness or value. The specific value types represented by the value realms are related to the idea of value-in-general in that they all deal with things, events, persons fulfilling concepts.

Psychological Value

The "good" of psychological functioning is the fulfillment by persons of concepts such as motivation, feeling, and attitude. Psychological valuing is determining how or to what degree persons fulfill psychological functions. Expressions such as *I like . . . , I prize . . . , I prefer . . .* , and the like are psychological applications of the general value term *good.*

Some value *statements* from the psychological value realm: "I like my work." "I prefer participatory sports." "I prize achievement." Such statements indicate that a person is valuing from the perspective of psychological value. Some psychological value *situations:* a person deciding the kinds of hobbies he likes, a person fulfilling her desire to be a success, a person exhibiting a preference for certain types of books. Some psychological value *questions:* "Where do I prefer to live?" "What type of friends do I prefer?" "What type of job would I like to have?" A psychological value *choice:* "What do I prize more, the peacefulness of the country or the hustle of city life?"

In this type of valuing, students are thinking about themselves and others as being or not being motivated—as having or not having feelings, attitudes, preferences, intentions, interests.

Psychological value consists in having motives, being motivated, showing emotions, exhibiting attitudes. Psychological disvalue consists in lacking motivation, being apathetic, being bored and uninterested.

Social Value

The "good" of group performance is the fulfillment by persons in groups of social concepts such as roles and norms. Social value is determined according to how well or to what degree persons fulfill the idea of group performance. The fulfillment of social duty and responsibility are included in the domain of social value. Social *duty* is the social interpretation of the *good* in general.

Various kinds of *statements* refer to social value or lack of it. "He is a good member of society" expresses the social "good." "He never does his job" indicates lack of social value. There are many different *situations* that illustrate social value—a person performing his job requirements, a person doing his duty as a citizen of his country, a person doing what is expected of him by his peers. Social value may be indicated by *questions:* example: "How well am I doing my job?" "Which expectations ought I to follow?" "Do I recognize my social obligations?" A value *choice* in this domain: "Should I do what my parents expect or what my friends expect?"

In this type of valuing students are viewing or thinking about themselves and others as conforming to social role expectations. The students see themselves as being responsive to social roles and norms. They determine how well they exemplify the concept of social functioning.

Socially valuable acts consist in doing one's job, doing one's duty, doing what is expected, keeping agreements and promises, adhering to contracts, being responsible. That which is not socially valuable consists in ignoring obligations, breaking promises, not doing one's job, avoiding responsibility, being delinquent.

Economic Value

The "good" of economic value is the fulfillment by things of economic concepts such as usefulness and scarcity. A useful thing is the more economically valuable the rarer it is. *Expensive* and *costly* are economic interpretations of the general value term *good*.

The *statement* "The object is rare and expensive" describes something that is economically valuable. A relative lack of economic value is expressed by "I won't pay $4,000 for that car—it is not worth it." Another statement indicating that which is economically valuable: "The irrigation project will make that land increase in price." There are many different *situations* that illustrate economic value, such as the wages a person can command on the labor market, the rising price of oil because of increasing scarcity, the rising prices of consumer items. A value *choice* in the economic domain might be selecting from several jobs the one that would provide the highest wage.

This type of valuing has students viewing or thinking about things as useful and scarce. The students conceptualize things in terms of their functions—as products. In addition they view useful things in terms of how available they are. They determine how things fulfill economic laws and theories.

The student considers that what is most economically valuable is that which is most useful and rare, that what is economically not valuable is that which is least useful and most available.

Ethical Value

The ethical "good" is the fulfillment by persons of ethical concepts such as the idea of the unique self, the idea of self-definition, the idea of self-improvement. The more a person fulfills his/her self-definition (self-concept), the more ethical that person is. The terms *honest, sincere, authentic* represent the ethical *good*—they are ethical applications of the idea of *good* in general.

Various *statements* refer to ethical value or lack of it. "He is authentic, honest, and sincere in whatever he does" expresses the ethical good. "He is not true to himself" indicates a lack of ethical value. Language of this type shows that a person is valuing within the ethical realm.

There are many different *situations* that illustrate ethical valuation: some examples are a student committing himself to a lifelong career, a parent caring for the development of a child, a person improving himself, a person fulfilling his promise. Ethical value is often indicated by the articulation of ethical *questions*, such as "What can I do to improve myself?" or "Am I really committed to this task?" or "Has he chosen well?" An ethical value *choice* presents alternatives to be selected—"Shall I commit myself to the improvement of my people or not?"

This value type has the students thinking about themselves and others as ethical persons—as persons who fulfill their chosen, unique self-concepts. The students will consider an ethical person one who is genuine, sincere, honest, one who has integrity and self-respect—a self-actualizing person, in Maslow's terms. An unethical person is one who is directed by others, who is not self-chosen, who is inauthentic, insincere, not true to himself.

Social-Ethical Value

The "good" of social ethics is the fulfillment by groups of persons of social ethical concepts such as group involvement and identity, group decision-making, group improvement. Social-ethical value is establishing group involvement and group decision-making. *We are a group, We are unified, We are together* are ideas that represent the social-ethical "good"—they are social-ethical applications of the idea "good" in general.

Specific kinds of statements express social-ethical value: "The union makes its own decisions." "That family acts as a unit." A lack of social-ethical value is indicated by these statements: "They are an oppressed people." "They have not achieved their independence." Many different social-ethical *situations* can be identified—the American colonies in their fight for independence, the development of a nation as an independent group of people, the continuity of a family group through generations. Some social-ethical *questions:* "Which is the best direction for the group?" "Are we a team?" A value *choice* in this realm is expressed by the question "Should the major goal of the United States be national defense or the rehabilitation of cities?"

In this type of valuing, students are thinking about themselves and others as persons involved with, participating in, and integrated in groups. Students conceptualize themselves and others as being involved in the norms, institutions, roles, goals, and symbols of a system of interacting persons—a group. The more a group fulfills its concept of its own decided-upon institutions, goals, norms, and symbols, the more socially ethical it is. The students consider the group as unique and special—establishing an identity and a unity of its own.

Esthetic Value

The "good" of esthetics is the enjoyment of beauty or special quality in things perceived and valued as unique, as having unity and singularity. *Beautiful, one-of-a-kind,* and *special* are a few esthetic applications of the general value term *good.*

The following are *statements* that express esthetic value or lack of it: "This blue vase is exquisite." "I find the mountains thrilling." "Litter makes the whole scene ugly." "That meal was food for the gods!" Esthetic valuing takes place in an infinite variety of *situations;* for example: viewing a famous painting, savoring really fine foods, landscaping a garden, listening to music. Some esthetic value questions: "Do you see that as beautiful?" "Does it give you a sense of elation or intensity or joy?" A value *choice* in this domain: "Which would give me the greatest enjoyment—seeing a Shakespeare play or going to a gourmet restaurant?"

In this kind of valuing, students are *involved* in things, *experience* them, viewing them as unique, special, one-of-a-kind. The student sees things in their totality or wholeness, determines that things exemplify esthetic concepts.

Esthetic value consists in viewing things imaginatively, in a special way, in a novel way, as beautiful. Esthetic value is lacking when things are seen as commonplace, ordinary, or ugly.

Poetic and Literary Value

Poetic or literary "good" is viewing words uniquely—as metaphors. Poetic value arises from words fulfilling the idea of uniqueness.

Some value *statements* from the poetic value realm: "Those words have a poetic ring." "That is a piece of literature." A poetic value *question:* "Does the novel provide an effective analogy?" An example of a poetic value *choice:* "Which set of metaphors expresses the intended meaning of the poem?"

This value type has students viewing words as metaphors—as unique, special, as unities, as experiences. Poetic value consists in viewing words imaginatively, creatively, metaphorically. Poetic value is lacking to the extent that language is treated analytically, formally, grammatically.

Technological Value

The "good" of technology is the fulfillment by things of technological concepts such as system, structure, relation. Technological value is determined according to whether or not a thing fulfills the idea of being structured or systematic. *It is engineered* and *It operates* are technological applications of the general value term *good*.

The following are *statements* that express technological value: "Everything is operational and ready to go." "The combat unit is a fighting machine." "All the pieces are in place and the rocket is set for launching." These are *situations* that are concerned with technological value: devising a system for using solar energy to produce electricity; designing a plane that is structurally sound. Technological value *questions* include "Is the mind nothing but a complex computer?" and "Has 20th-century society become a vast megamachine?" A value *choice* in this area: "Which type of technology can most easily be made operational?"

In technological valuing, the student is thinking about things as interrelated—as machines. The student sees things as mechanically operating, sees things from the perspective of parts and elements in various relationships such as balancing, turning, pulling, winding; judges things as fulfilling technological concepts.

The student considers as technologically valuable those things which are engineered, which work, which operate; as technologically not valuable, those things which are inoperative.

Legal Value

The "good" of the law is the fulfillment of legal concepts by interacting persons. An important legal concept is the idea of lawful regulation of interpersonal and intergroup relationships. Legal value is determined according to whether or not relationships conform to the law. *It is legal* and *It is within the law* are ideas representing the legal *good*—legal applications of the general idea of *good*.

These are value *statements* from the legal value realm: "Freedom of speech is guaranteed by the Constitution." "It is against the law to discriminate by race or sex in hiring practices." Some legal value *situations* include upholding a person's constitutional rights, and adhering to the notion of being an equal-opportunity employer. A legal value *question:* "Is the corporation guilty of violating the antitrust laws? A value choice: "Should I obey the law?"

In legal valuing, the student is viewing persons and groups of persons in systematic relationship—that is, as following formal rules and principles (The Law). Students view groups as operating within a formal system—as constitutional, lawful, legal. They judge persons and groups of persons as to whether they fulfill legal concepts.

INTERRELATIONS OF THE VALUE REALMS

Each of the value realms has its own specific value. Together they give alternative value perspectives. Indeed, valuing is generally the harmonizing of alternative value perspectives. The more a person values from each of the different perspectives the more of a valuing person he or she will be. The valuing person is an enriched person, a fuller person, a person who has greater meaning. That person will not be one who is value-blind or limited in his value perspective.

The following are typical *statements* expressing some interrelationships of the value realms. "I am expected to do it but I don't like it" expresses an interrelation between psychological and social values. "A person should not be sold into slavery" implies an interrelationship between ethical and economic values. "The Picasso is priceless" expresses a relationship between esthetic and economic values. There are many different *situations* that involve value interrelationships. For example: a person selecting a career that he feels he ought to pursue even though he expects to gain little financial reward; a person obeying the law even though he does not like it. An illustration of a value *dilemma* among the value realms: "I would like this job because it is very well suited to me, but this other one would pay a lot more."

Valuing from the perspectives of the different realms will have students thinking about the world from more than one value perspective. They will have many different value frameworks from which to view the world. They will be aware of the relationships and tensions between the different value perspectives. They will be aware of the "values" of each of the value realms.

THE VALUE DIMENSIONS

Value in general has three distinct dimensions which are interrelated. These dimensions are practical value, intrinsic value, and technical value.

The *practical* value dimension deals with things as items in a class; they are valued according to class properties they possess. *Intrinsic* value deals with things as unique entitites; they are valued as special, one-of-a-kind. *Technical* value deals with things by means of mental construction; they are valued in terms of a logical structure applied to them.

A person can deal with anything intrinsically by involving himself with it, practically by viewing it as a member of a class, technically by means of logical or formal construction.

Intrinsic Value—The Value of Involvement

The intrinsic "good" is the fulfillment of unique ideas. A unique idea is a unity, a Gestalt, a singularity. The value derived from things exemplifying unique ideas is the value of uniqueness and involvement. The terms *unique, special, one-of-a-kind, individual* represent the intrinsic "good." *Delight, joy, beauty, intrinsic satisfaction, peak experience, exalted experience* also refer to intrinsic value. This kind of value has been variously characterized as the "Aha!" experience; as seeing the totality of something at a glance; as insight, vision, or illumination; as shock of recognition; as ecstasy.

These are *statements* expressing intrinsic value: "It is a once-in-a-lifetime experience." "What a joyful occasion!" Intrinsic value *situations:* a person deriving great joy from accomplishment; a person involved with his or her work; two people in love; a person committing himself or herself to a lifelong career. An illustration of a *question* in the intrinsic value area: "How involved should I get with this person?" A *choice* involving intrinsic value is expressed by the question "Whom do I choose to marry and be with for the rest of my life—Jane or Martha?"

Intrinsic valuing has the student viewing things in a unique way—thinking of things as special, one-of-a-kind, and particular, as unities and totalities that are infinitely rich in qualities, as involvements and immediate experiences. Things which fulfill or exemplify unique concepts are experienced as singularities, infinities, Gestalts. Intrinsic value is lacking to the extent that things are treated analytically, or viewed as commonplace or ordinary, or with indifference.

Practical Value

The practical "good" is the fulfillment of class concepts. Things are considered as members of classes. Things in a class have properties in common with other things in the class. If a thing corresponds to its class concept, having all the properties its name implies, it is considered a "good" thing. The practical "good" is represented by the terms *good, fine, excellent, great,* and the like. Practical valuing is that of everyday pragmatic thinking. One can judge anything in a practical way by classifying it and determining the extent to which it exemplifies class properties. A thing is good, fair, poor, or no good, in terms of practical value, depending on how completely its characteristics conform to the full idea of the kind of thing it is.

These are practical value *statements:* "That is a fine watch." "Lincoln was a great President." "He's just a fair performer." "This steak is not so good." Practical value *situations* would include reviewing a play to judge its quality and the ranking of a student on the basis of his performance. Illustrations of practical value *questions:* "How good is that car?" "Which is the vintage wine?" A value *choice* in this dimension is expressed by the question "Which is the better community—Fairborn or Greenboro?"

In practical valuing, students relate things to practical or class concepts. They judge things in terms of how fully they exemplify their class concepts—from good (having all the properties of the concept) to fair (lacking some of the properties) to no good (lacking most of the properties).

Technical and Scientific Value

The technical "good" is the fulfillment of technical ideas—mental constructs, logical entities, formal relations. Technical ideas are often expressed as definitions, models, charts, laws, formulas, and the like. Examples of logical entities are the idea of twoness and the definition of velocity as distance divided by time. The terms *structure, system, logical, formal, precise,* and *perfect* represent the technical "good."

Some value *statements* from the technical domain: "The human body is a highly structured system." "That mathematical formula is a precise definition." Some technical value *situations* might involve consideration of the relationship between the moon and the tides, the relationship of the elements in the formula H_2O, the structure of the DNA molecule, the solar system, the structure of a corporation, the American economic system. Examples of technical value *questions:* "Does the theory apply?" "Is this H_2O?" A technical value *choice* might be expressed by the question "Which structural design would best implement the specifications of the plane?"

In determining technical value, students are viewing or thinking about things as structured, ordered, logical. The student learns to contrast such things, which fulfill or exemplify technical concepts, with those which are considered unstructured, random, unrelated, unsystematic.

THE VALUE REALMS AND DIMENSIONS

The application of the three value dimensions to persons, groups, and things produces a typology of the various value realms. (The chart presented below is an adaptation of Hartman's more elaborate typology.)

Typology of Value Realms[2]

Applied to	Intrinsic Value	Practical Value	Technical Value
Persons	Ethical value	Psychological value	Legal value
Groups of persons	Social-ethical value	Social value	Legal value
Things	Esthetic and poetic value	Economic value	Technological and scientific value

Intrinsic value applied to persons yields the realm of ethical value; applied to groups, social-ethical value; applied to things, esthetic value. Intrinsic value is that of involvement and is viewed as having infinities of richness and meaning.

Practical value applied to persons yields the realm of psychological value; applied to groups, social value; applied to things, economic value. Practical values are those of the everyday pragmatic world.

Technical value applied to interpersonal or intergroup relations yields the realm of legal value; applied to things, technological and scientific value. Technical values are those of precision, structure, system.

---

[2]From *The Structure of Value: Foundations of Scientific Axiology* by Robert S. Hartman (p. 311). Copyright © 1967 by Southern Illinois University Press. Reprinted by permission of the Southern Illinois University Press.

APPLIED VALUE TERMS

There are various words and phrases that people commonly use to discuss various kinds of value. The following chart shows some terms that indicate the "good," "valuable," or "worthwhile" in each of the value disciplines, and also their opposites.

Value Discipline	Terms indicating the "good" of the discipline	Terms indicating its absence or opposite
Ethical Value	sincere honest genuine being oneself	insincere dishonest inauthentic feigning
Esthetic Value	beautiful special imaginative	ugly mediocre ordinary
Social-Ethical Value	independence freedom liberty	oppression coercion enslavement
Poetic & Literary Value	poetic metaphorical literary	prosaic/analytic literal expository
Psychological Value	motivated interested goal-directed	listless bored indifferent
Social Value	dutiful doing a job	anomie alienation
Economic Value	expensive costly	inexpensive cheap
Technological Value	mechanical engineered	inoperative thrown together
Legal Value	lawful constitutional	lawless illegal

USING THE VALUE ACTIVITIES

Each chapter in Part II and Part III of this book presents activities teachers may use to encourage students to value in the various realms and dimensions of value. Each activity consists of the following elements:

A statement of *purpose*, in terms of expected student outcomes.

A statement of the *meaning*, or central conception, explored in the activity, in terms of the type of value involved.

A basic or core *procedure* providing materials and instructions for student activities, and related value *questions* for discussion.

Materials and/or suggestions for one or more additional related activities, requiring the student to (a) formulate an appropriate value *statement*, (b) deal with a value *situation*, (c) present a value *argument*, (d) make a value *choice*, or (e) confront a value *dilemma*.

An *evaluation* procedure whereby the teacher may assess whether the purpose of the lesson has been achieved.

Sequencing

Each chapter in Part II provides a variety of activities in one of the value realms—psychological, social, economic, ethical, social-ethical, esthetic, poetic, legal, or technological. For the materials to be most effective, students should engage in enough activities to acquire understanding of a particular value realm before moving on to another. However, the teacher may decide how to sequence these chapters, how to order the activities within a given chapter, and how to select the part or parts of an activity to use at a given time. (The activities are numbered merely for purposes of convenient reference.)

The activities in Part III require students to contrast, compare, and make judgements or choices among the various value realms and dimensions. These chapters should be dealt with after all of the individual value realms have been developed.

Curriculum Placement

The activities may be effectively used in various subject areas. For example, they are obviously suitable in the social studies program, where valuing and value choices are integral. They may also be used in the language arts area, where they provide a needed opportunity for teachers to promote familiarity with and effective use of the language of valuing.

The materials can work well in special programs for the gifted. One of the fundamental characteristics of gifted students is their high degree of interest and ability in valuing.

Different types of values may be emphasized in different areas. Literature classes might use the Poetic Value activities. Science teachers might use some of the activities in the Technical Value dimension. Economics teachers may use the Economic Value activities. The materials may also be used in guidance and self-development courses.

It is possible and might be desirable to promote a special time slot for value development. This could be done, for example, in the elementary school by setting aside 20 to 30 minutes two to three times a week. On the junior high and high school levels, special half-year courses might be established.

Adaptability of Activities

Many of the activities in this book are adaptable, by teachers, for almost any age and ability level, and for groups or individual students. The teacher should not hesitate to modify or reconstruct activities in order to make them meaningful to a particular class, group, or individual student. Any of the activities may be regarded as a model that the teacher can use to generate other activities for particular students given their specific abilities, talents, interests, and needs.

PART II

Activities in the Various Value Realms

Chapter 2

PSYCHOLOGICAL VALUE:
Motives, Attitudes, and
Feelings

Students can value themselves and others as psychologically functioning persons, by applying psychological concepts such as motivation, emotion, and attitude. In performing psychological valuation, students establish a psychological concept such as motivation and judge themselves or others to determine how they exemplify the concept.

Psychological value is fulfillment of psychological functions. Words such as *motivated, prizing, desiring, liking, favoring,* and *interest* indicate psychological values; *unmotivated, bored,* and *listless* indicate lack of such value.

This chapter presents activities that will encourage students to value themselves and others as motivated, feeling persons. Students will be helped to become aware of their motivations, to set priorities among motives, and to improve motivational performance.

1. "I LIKE . . ."

Purpose: To have students give instances of how they exemplify the idea of motivation.

Meaning: Persons may be viewed as fulfilling specific motives (expressed in terms of liking, wanting, being interested in, etc.).

Procedures:

A. *Orientation*

Give students a list of specific activities and goals and have them check the things they like or want.

Wear nice clothes ____	Be an engineer ____
Play baseball ____	Make good grades ____
Ride a bike ____	Be rich ____
Play the piano ____	Help other people ____
Read novels ____	Be famous ____
Draw pictures ____	Dance ____
Eat pizza ____	Cook ____
Sing in the choir ____	Listen to music ____
Do puzzles ____	Talk with friends ____
Watch TV ____	Go camping ____
Write poems ____	Be a cheerleader ____

Then have the students indicate things they like or want by writing in the blanks of incomplete sentences. Some things could be the same as items in the list, or suggested by them, but the idea is for students to think of other things and to match them to the expressions used in the sentences. Students should look up or ask about words they don't know.

1. I like _____ very much.
2. I like _____ fairly well.
3. I like _____ sometimes.
4. I like _____ a little.
5. I love to _____ .
6. I like to _____ .
7. I enjoy _____ .
8. I have an appetite for _____ .
9. I have a hankering for _____ .

10. I am inclined to _____ .
11. I am in favor of _____..
12. I am very much interested in _____ .
13. I have a desire to _____ .
14. I want to _____ .
15. I am fascinated by _____ .
16. I am drawn to _____ .
17. I get a kick out of _____ .
18. I have a craving for _____ .
19. I get a charge out of _____ .
20. I am driven to _____ .

B. *Vocabulary*
   1. Have students look up the meanings and derivations of *motive*, *motion*, and *emotion*.
   2. Give students a list of character traits and have them indicate whether each term describes a highly motivated person (+) or one who is not motivated (0). Examples:

dull	enthusiastic	animated
vigorous	spirited	zestless
curious	bored	lively
listless	apathetic	lethargic
active	spunky	inspired
lazy	eager	

Value Questions For Discussion

1. What specific things are you *most* interested in? Which would you work hard to achieve?
2. Should everybody like or want the same things?
3. Are there some things everybody is enthusiastic about?
4. How can you tell whether someone really wants something?

Value Situations

Students might do some or all of the following.
   1. Role-play one of these situations:
      a. You are motivated to ask a friend for a date.
      b. You are motivated to buy a new bicycle. You must ask your parents for the money.

2. Find some advertisements that attempt to motivate people to want certain things or do certain things.
3. Make stick-figure drawings of an active, enthusiastic person and a dull, zestless character.
4. Tell about some things you like best in one or more of these categories: Sports; Music; Books; Hobbies; TV Shows.

Evaluation: Have the students list 5 motives they have.

---

2. "I DISLIKE . . ."

Purpose: To have students give instances of the non-fulfillment of the idea of motivation.

Meaning: Lack of motivation is psychological disvalue. Of course, a lack of this or that specific motive is not necessarily a failure in motivation; but to have no or almost no motivation at all indicates an extreme degree of motivational failure.

Procedure: Have the students complete sentences such as the following to indicate things they dislike and things they don't care about.

1. I dislike _____ at all times.
2. I dislike _____ sometimes.
3. I am lazy about _____ .
4. I am bored with _____ .
5. I have no appetite for _____ .
6. I don't have any interest in _____ .
7. I hate _____ .
8. I have an aversion to _____ .
9. It is no use trying to _____ .
10. It is not worth while to _____ .
11. I am disgusted with _____ .
12. I do not want to _____ .
13. It's too much trouble to _____ .
14. Why should I _____ .
15. I don't care about _____ .

Value Questions For Discussion

1. Describe some behaviors that show lack of specific motivations.
2. Name something someone else likes but you are not motivated toward, or vice versa.
3. Are there some things everyone hates and tries to avoid or prevent? Some things that bore everyone?
4. If something bores you, should you necessarily try to get interested in it? If you dislike something, should you try to like it?
5. If *everything* bores you, is that a problem?

Value Situations

Students might role-play the following situations:
1. You are babysitting with a child who does not want to do anything. Try to get him interested in something.
2. You are a teacher trying to get an unmotivated student interested in a school subject.

Value Statement

Have the students write a sentence or story about a person who is not motivated. Encourage them to use a variety of synonyms for "not motivated."

Evaluation: Have the students name 3 specific things they are not motivated toward.

---

3. WHEN AND HOW MOTIVES ARE USEFUL

Purpose: To have students give instances of persons fulfilling the idea of functional motivation.

Meaning: Having a particular motive may be especially useful or appropriate in certain situations and not in others.

Procedure: Ask the students to write about times when it would be useful or appropriate to have the motives listed here.

Helpful	Calm
Forceful	Cheerful
Agreeable	Cautious
Disagreeable	Fearful
Angry	

Value Questions For Discussion

1. How might some of the listed motives be useful?
2. Can you think of times when it is out of context or not useful to have a certain motive—when another would be more appropriate?
3. Give an example from history or literature of a person who was lacking in a motive that would have been useful.

Value Argument

Have the students defend a position that a certain motive is useful to them in a particular circumstance.

Value Situation

Have the students identify some motives that are particularly appropriate for (a) a government leader, (b) a businessman, (c) a teacher.

Evaluation: Have the students give 3 instances of when the motive of fear might be useful.

———————————

4. THE VALUE OF USEFUL MOTIVES

Purpose: To have students give instances of persons fulfilling the idea of functional motivation.

Meaning: Some motives tend to be useful and functional more often or more generally than others.

Procedure: Have each student rank these motives in order according to which are the best (most often useful) motives for getting along in the practical world:

To be neat	To be clean
To be shy	To be angry
To be fearful	To be kind
To be a bully	To be anxious
To be thrifty	To be friendly
To be brave	To help others
To be curious	To be jealous

Value Questions For Discussion

1. Which motives would be useful to you in almost any situation?
2. Which motives are useful to you least often or never?
3. Can you think of any motives that would not be useful in most situations but might be useful in some situations?
4. When did you lack a useful motive in a particular situation? Could you do better now?

Value Argument

Have two students select particular motives and each try to prove that the motive selected is the most useful one in a given situation.

Evaluation: Ask the students to identify a motive that would be useful in each of the following situations:

1. Playing football.
2. Visiting a friend in the hospital.
3. Going on vacation.

---

5. TYPES OF MOTIVES

Purpose: To have students identify persons exemplifying motives in the five important categories of safety, belongingness, self-respect, self-development, and physiological well-being.

Meaning: Abraham Maslow has developed a classification of motives into five general categories. Persons may or may not be aware of these categories or exemplify motivation of all these types.

Procedure: Have the students identify some of their specific motives in each of the categories below.

1. *Physiological or health needs.*
   What appetites do you have? What tastes and smells do you like?
   What health needs are you interested in? (E.g.: nutrition, exercise, rest, clean air, etc.)
2. *Safety motives.*
   When do you feel the need for safety?
3. *Belongingness and love and affection* (giving and receiving love).
   When do you want to have a sense of belongingness?
   Who do you want to love you?
4. *Self-respect.*
   Respect from others: When and from whom do you want attention and praise?
   Achievement: What would you like to achieve?
5. *Self-development.*
   What do you like to do that you do well or might do well?

Value Questions For Discussion

1. Name some specific safety motives that you have or should have.
2. Name some health motives that you have or should have. (Continue in the same manner to discuss other categories of motives.)

Value Situation

Have the students tell how they are motivated to follow safety rules in the following instances:

    a. On a boat.
    b. Driving a car.
    c. Swimming.
    d. Working in a kitchen.

Evaluation: Have the students name a safety motive, a belongingness motive, and a self-respect motive.

6. PSYCHOLOGICAL "OUGHT"

Purpose: To have students identify non-fulfillment of functional motivation and think about ways of improving motivation.

Meaning: Psychological "ought" indicates a lacking in motivational performance—a person's motives are not varied enough, or strong enough, or are not suitable for the person or situation. Psychological "ought" indicates improvements needed in motivation.

Procedure: Have the students write answers to the following questions.

What are some short-term interests you ought to develop?
What are some long-term interests you ought to develop?
What are some interests you ought to develop in the future?
What are some interests you might develop that can be helpful to others?

Value Questions For Discussion

1. What are some things one might do to improve motivational performance (develop more interests or more suitable goals or pursue aims more actively)?
2. Name some interests that some well-known persons ought to develop.

Value Situations

Encourage students to do the following:

1. Observe some highly motivated people in action. Describe their activities.
2. Read a biography of some highly motivated person.

Value Argument

Have the students write or tell about a situation in which one of the following persons is not suitably motivated and ought to be better motivated: (*a*) a student, (*b*) a team player, (*c*) an employee.

Evaluation: Have the students identify one or more specific interests that someone in public life ought to develop and suggest ways of developing each interest.

7. WHAT STOPS ME FROM BEING MOTIVATED?

Purpose: To have students think about what it means to be blocked from exemplifying useful motives.

Meaning: A psychological "good" is for persons to be motivated in useful ways. Blocks to having useful motives ought to be overcome.

Procedure: Have the students tell what stops them from being fully motivated in each of the following areas.

What stops me from being . . .

Friendly?_____

Responsible?_____

Happy?_____

Forceful?_____

Skillful?_____

Trusting?_____

Caring?_____

Value Questions For Discussion:

1. What stops people from having certain motives?
2. How can these blocks be overcome?

Evaluation: Have the students list 2 things that stop them from being motivated.

Chapter 3

SOCIAL VALUE:
Role Expectations, Norms, Social Duty

Students can value themselves and others as socially functioning persons: they can think of themselves and others as functioning in groups, as fulfilling social roles and norms. In social valuation, students establish a social concept (role expectation, norm, institution) and judge persons to determine whether they fulfill the concept.

Social value is the fulfillment, by persons or groups of persons, of specific role expectations, norms, and institutions. Words such as *duty, commitment, responsibility, co-operation, obligation* are among those used to refer to what is socially valuable. *Deviant, delinquent, alienation, anomie, desertion, avoiding responsibility* are often used to indicate social disvalue—lack or opposite of social value.

Social value judgements emerge from the application of theories and concepts of the discipline of sociology. The key or central concepts are derived from social theories such as those of Talcott Parsons or Robert Merton.

This section presents activities that will help students become aware of social roles and responsibilities—their own as well as others. Students will also be encouraged to improve their own performance in such roles and responsibilities.

31

8. FULFILLING SOCIAL ROLES

Purpose: To have students identify examples of the fulfillment and non-fulfillment of social roles by persons.

Meaning: Role expectations are sets of rules that guide people's actions in social roles. When a person does what is expected of him in a role he is fulfilling his role. An important aspect of social value is the fulfillment of role expectations.

Procedure: Have the students complete value statements. Examples:

1. I expect_____as a consumer.
2. I expect_____when I marry.
3. I expect_____from a policeman.
4. I expect_____from a doctor.
5. I expect_____from my parents.
6. I expect_____from my teacher.
7. My parents expect_____of me.
8. My teacher expects_____of me.
9. My friend expects_____of me.
10. We expect_____of the principal.
11. We expect_____of the mayor.
12. We expect_____of the president.
13. I am a tenant and I expect_____from the landlord. The landlord expects_____of me.
14. I am a citizen. It is my duty to _____ .
    It is the duty of the government to_____ .
15. I am a football coach. It is my job to _____ .
    It is the team's job to _____ .
16. I am a patient. I am obligated to _____ .
    The doctor is obligated to'_____ .
17. I am a pilot. I must _____ .
    The control tower operators must _____ .
18. I am a writer. I agree to _____ .
    The publisher agrees to _____ .
19. I am married. I promise to _____ .
    My spouse promises to _____ .
20. I am a builder. I have a contract to _____ .
    My customers have a contract to _____ .

21. I am the flying member of a high wire team. I co-ordinate my actions so that _____ .
The catcher co-ordinates his actions so that _____ .
22. I am a member of a doubles tennis team. I integrate my actions in such a way that _____ .
My partner integrates his actions so that _____ .

Value Questions For Discussion

1. Do you expect others to fulfill their roles? Why?
2. What are some expectations you have of others? What are some expectations that others have of you?

Value Situations

Have the students write some role expectations for each of the following relationships.

employee/employer	doctor/nurse
buyer/seller	judge/lawyer
teacher/student	pilot/co-pilot

Value Statements

Have the students write statements using the following words as synonyms for role expectations.

promise	oath
obligation	responsibility
duty	commitment

Evaluation: Have the student list 5 ways in which a congressman might fulfill his role.

9. SOCIAL DISVALUE

Purpose: To have students indicate instances of social disvalue.

Meaning: Non-fulfillment of social norms and expectations is social disvalue.

Procedure: Have students complete statements such as these, about failure to do what was expected of them.

1. I withdrew from _____. (an obligation) (E.g.: ". . . from my obligation to clean my room.")
2. I ignored _____. (a promise)
3. I rejected _____. (an offer)
4. I did not abide by _____. (a vow)
5. I ignored _____. (a request)
6. I was lax in _____. (my job)
7. I avoided _____. (a responsibility)
8. I shirked _____. (a duty)
9. I deserted _____. (a post)

Value Questions For Discussion

1. What are some expectations you have not lived up to?
2. Can you think of public or fictional persons who have failed to fulfill expectations over long periods of time?

Value Statements

Students might do one or more of the following things.

1. Write a description about each of the following showing how they disregard social norms and expectations.

a hobo	a delinquent
a hermit	a truant
a bohemian	a criminal

2. The phrases below illustrate social disvalue—use the phrases in an account.

   "Do not recognize obligations to anyone"
   "Fell down on the job"
3. Take a character from literature and describe his or her alienation.

Evaluation: Have the student give 3 instances of a person ignoring social expectations.

10. AVOIDING EXPECTATIONS

Purpose: To have students identify examples of non-fulfillment of expectations.

Meaning: Non-fulfillment of expectations is social disvalue.

Procedure: Have students indicate which of the following rules or expectations they would always follow (+), and which ones they might *not* follow at times (0).

___No Fishing

___Don't Walk

___No Trespassing

___No Skating

___High Voltage

___Beware of Dogs

___Don't Litter

___No Exit

___Prevent Fires

___Quiet! Hospital Area

___Up Escalator

___Do Not Enter

___In

___Out

___Wet Cement

___No Swimming

___Railroad Crossing

___Wet Paint!

Value Questions For Discussion

1. Are there times when you do not follow community rules or expectations?
2. Name some rules that you either do or do not follow (*a*) at school, (*b*) in the library, (*c*) at a baseball game, (*d*) in a department store, (*e*) while riding a bicycle.

Value Statements

Have the students write an account of a time when they avoided one of the following.

Paying a debt.

Household chores.

Library fines.

Homework.

Co-operation in groups.

Going to school.

Evaluation: Have students write about 3 social rules they have broken and 3 social rules they have followed.

11. FULFILLING MUTUAL ROLE EXPECTATIONS

Purpose: To have students determine the extent to which they fulfill the expectations of others.

Meaning: People may or may not fulfill expectations others have of them. Fulfilling expectations is an aspect of social value.

Procedure: Invite the students to draw stick figures representing persons in reciprocal roles, such as doctor/patient, teacher/student, parent/child, buyer/seller, etc. Then have the students draw speech balloons and write value statements indicating what each expects of the other.

Value Questions For Discussion

1. What are some expectations that people in such relationships (doctor/patient, teacher/student, etc.) might have of each other?
2. Give instances of when these people fulfill each other's expectations and when they do not.

Value Situation

Students might role-play one or more of the following situations.
1. A patient not doing what the doctor expects.
2. A student not doing what the teacher expects.
3. A child not doing what a parent expects.
4. A buyer not doing what a seller expects.

Evaluation: Have the student give 3 instances that illustrate his or her non-fulfillment of someone else's expectations.

12. REWARD AND PUNISHMENT

Purpose: To have students determine the extent to which they respond to social rewards and punishments.

Meaning: Social sanctions (rewards and punishments) are given for conformity and non-conformity to social norms and rules. Persons may or may not respond to or be reinforced by such rewards and punishments.

Procedure: Give students the following list and have them determine who is and who is not being reinforced by social rewards and punishments in each situation.

1. A person who saves money in the bank knowing he will be paid interest.
2. A person passing a red light knowing he may get a ticket.
3. A person working in order to receive a paycheck.
4. A student performing well in school in order to get high grades.
5. A child cleaning his room so that he can go out to play.
6. A person performing well in a job in order to get a promotion.

Value Questions For Discussion

1. In the above situations, which rewards and punishments are the people responding to and which are they not responding to?
2. In cases where people are ignoring a potential reward or punishment, might they respond to some different one?

Value Statements

Have the students write about some types of rewards and punishments that were given in the past to encourage people to conform to laws and customs, and have them indicate whether or not they think those rewards and punishments would get poeple to respond to social rules today.

Evaluation: Have students name 3 rewards and 3 punishments that they have responded to at home by following rules.

13. FULFILLING ROLE EXPECTATIONS

Purpose: To have students judge how well persons fulfill role expectations.

Meaning: Role performance may be judged by comparing it to role expectations.

Procedure: Have the students read the expectations (requirements) listed below for the roles of "Assistant Director of Volunteers" and "Gift Shop Manager" in a hospital. Then have the students role-play interviewing one another for the jobs. Have one student play the part of the interviewer and other students play the parts of applicants for the job. The interviewer must determine whether each person seeking the job would be able to meet the requirements. The interviewer must ask appropriate questions (e.g.: "Can you type?" "Can you write letters?" "Have you ever prepared a budget?" "How would you go about getting new volunteers?"). The interviewer must also make a final judgement as to who would best fulfill the job requirements and should therefore be hired.

Assistant Director of Volunteers

Recruits, interviews, and screens volunteers.
Orients them to hospital; trains them for jobs.
Maintains job schedules; calls replacements or substitutes when necessary.
Handles correspondence.
Types; files.
Takes charge of volunteers' uniforms.
Makes coffee; buys supplies for volunteers.

Gift Shop Manager

Prepares annual budget and report for the women's auxilary.
Buys merchandise.
Originates displays of merchandise throughout hospital, as well as in shop itself.
Supervises gift-and-candy cart (stocking, scheduling, route, etc.).
Supervises volunteer sales staff.
Keeps books.
Takes inventory; does stock work; sells.

Value Questions For Discussion

1. According to the job requirements presented, which persons interviewed seemed most able to fulfill the requirements?
2. Which persons seemed least able? Which requirements do you think they would not be able to fulfill?
3. Did the interviewer ask the right questions?

Value Situation

Present a list of roles to the students and have them determine some people who are qualified to fulfill those roles. Examples:
President, Senator, Principal, Captain of school team

Evaluation: Have the students name 2 roles that they could perform well, and list 3 requirements they can fulfill for each role.

---

14. RANKING ROLE PERFORMANCE

Purpose: To have students rank their performance in various roles, on a scale that ranges from *good* to *no good*.

Meaning: Role performance may be ranked or judged in a range of values from *good* to *fair* to *poor* to *no good*.

Procedure: Give the students a chart like the one below and have them select some roles they perform and rank their own performance in each such role by checking the appropriate box.

Role	*Role Performance*			
Consumer	Good____	Fair____	Poor____	No Good____
Club member	Good____	Fair____	Poor____	No Good____
Friend	Good____	Fair____	Poor____	No Good____
Student	Good____	Fair____	Poor____	No Good____
Host/Hostess	Good____	Fair____	Poor____	No Good____
Leader	Good____	Fair____	Poor____	No Good____
Traveler	Good____	Fair____	Poor____	No Good____

(Continued)

Brother/Sister	Good____	Fair____	Poor____	No Good____
Son/Daughter	Good____	Fair____	Poor____	No Good____
Community member	Good____	Fair____	Poor____	No Good____

Value Questions For Discussion

1. In which roles do you perform well? What are the role requirements that you fulfill?
2. Which roles do you not perform well in? What role requirements are you not able to fulfill?

Value Situation

Have the students rank various persons' role performance. Examples: service people in the community, government officials, news reporters, doctors.

Evaluation: Select a role that you think you perform well, and list 3 role requirements that you fulfill.

---

15. VALUING ACHIEVEMENT

Purpose: To have students identify instances of the fulfillment of achievement roles.

Meaning: An *achievement role* is a role in which excellence of performance is the criterion for judging effectiveness in the role. An achievement role is in contrast to an *ascribed role*, in which expectations are fulfilled by inherent qualities such as age, sex, etc.

Procedure: Have the students use a chart like the following to select and describe specific outstanding performances (past or present) by persons in various fields.

Field of Achievement	*Person Who Achieved*	*Specific Achievement*
Sports		
Medicine		
Law		
Education		
News reporting		
Entertainment		
Anthropology		
Science		
Aviation		

Value Questions For Discussion

1. What abilities and performances are required in order to fulfill the achievement roles described?
2. What are some things that would disqualify or prevent a person from achievement in a role?

Value Statement

Have the students show that a particular person is achieving in a role.

Evaluation: List 3 specific role performances that show achievement in a role.

---

16. SOCIAL "OUGHT" (1)

Purpose: To have students identify non-fulfillment in role performance and to suggest ways of improving role performance.

Meaning: Social "ought" indicates non-fulfillment of role expectations, and improvements needed in role performance.

Procedure: Ask the students to describe in written statements what each of the following persons "ought" to do to perform their job.

A student with low grades.
A homeowner who does not maintain his home.
An actor who forgets his lines.
A chef who can cook only a few dishes.

Value Questions

1. How ought a person perform in his or her job?
2. Are there some ways in which you are not doing a good job? What ought you to do?

Value Situation

Have students role-play one or more of the following situations.

1. A traffic policeman not performing his job well.
2. A baseball player in a slump.
3. A waitress who is doing her job poorly.

Then ask the students to role-play what "ought" to be accomplished by the above persons in order to fully fulfill their roles.

Evaluation: Have the students select a role and list 3 ways that a person in the role might improve his or her role performance.

---

17. SOCIAL "OUGHT" (2)

Purpose: To have students identify what they "ought" to do to improve their role performance.

Meaning: A person ought to perform well in fulfilling his social role expectations.

Procedure: Give students a chart like the following and have them describe in written statements, using the categories of the chart, what aspects of the role of *student* they are not fulfilling as well as they ought. They are to make suggestions of specific actions they might take to improve their role performance as students.

Improving My Performance as a Student

Organizing time:

_____

Study habits:

_____

Library skills:

_____

Listening skills:

_____

Taking tests:

_____

Improving reading materials:

_____

Asking appropriate questions:

_____

Getting along with people at school:

_____

Value Questions For Discussion

1. What are some things you ought to do to fully fulfill your role as a student?
2. Is it important for you to perform as well as you can as a student? Why?

Value Situations

Have the students do the following.

1. List ways to improve in your role as a friend.
2. List ways to improve in your role as a team or club member.
3. List ways to improve in your role as a son or daughter.

Evaluation: Have the students list 3 actions they ought to take to improve their role performance as students.

44

18. THE VALUE OF FRIENDSHIP

Purpose: To have students identify instances of the fulfillment of involvement roles.

Meaning: The role of *friend* is a type of social role. However, it is a special type of role which requires intrinsic involvement. It requires that the role participants treat each other as special, unique, particular.

Procedure: The teacher (or a student) may draw stick figures on the chalkboard to represent two people fulfilling the role of friends. Then have students use speech balloons to indicate what each friend expects of the other.

Value Questions For Discussion
1. What are some things that friends expect of each other?
2. Do any of the expectations require a special type of involvement or closeness?

Value Situation
Have the students describe the forms of personal involvement required of people in some of the following roles.

mother/child   grandparents/grandchildren
best friends   father/child

Evaluation: Have the students list 5 role actions that show involvement with a friend.

Chapter 4

ECONOMIC VALUE:
Goods, Work, and Consumption

Students can value things economically, by applying economic categories to things. Two important economic concepts are usefulness and scarcity. In performing economic valuation, students judge things to determine whether or how they exemplify such concepts.

Economic value is the fulfillment of economic concepts. Things are more economically valuable the more useful and scarce they are. Terms such as *expensive, costly, rare,* and *high-priced* are often used to indicate that which is economically valuable; *inexpensive, cheap,* and *abundant* refer to what is not economically valuable.

The application of economic theories (such as those of J. M. Keynes, for example) is the basis of economic value. Things are judged in relation to the theories and concepts of the discipline of economics.

This chapter presents activities that will encourage students to value things as useful or functional. The activities will also assist students to view goods and services in terms of their availability and their cost.

19. THE VALUE OF "GOODS"

Purpose: To have students identify things that have use value—
"goods."

Meaning: The valuation of things as having functions (as being useful) leads to economic value. The objects thus regarded are "goods."

Procedure: Ask the students to list as many objects as they can that would be of use to persons in the following roles.

pilot	sailor
farmer	auto mechanic
doctor	carpenter
fire fighter	mountain climber

Value Questions For Discussion

1. Name some things that are useful for various jobs.
2. Name some things that have little or no use.
3. Name some things that have no use value now but may have use in the future.
4. Name some things that had little use value in the past but have great use value today.

Value Situations

Ask the students to do the following.

1. Find out when people first began to see the usefulness of (*a*) metal, (*b*) the wheel, (*c*) raising crops, (*d*) domesticating animals.
2. Tell how the following things were useful in their time.
   The bow and arrow
   The Kentucky long rifle
   The cotton gin
   The Conestoga wagon

Evaluation: Have the students name 10 things that have use value in a modern city.

20. USEFULNESS OF "GOODS"

Purpose: To have students determine whether or not things fulfill the idea of usefulness.

Meaning: The "good" of economic value is usefulness of things. The objects thus regarded are "goods."

Procedure: Have the students name as many useful objects as they can for each of the following categories.

Telling time
Writing
Giving light
Building
Communication

Value Questions For Discussion

1. Name some objects that are useful in each of the listed categories. What useful qualities do the things have?
2. Name some objects that have a minimum of use.

Value Situation

Have the students select a product and tell how it is useful for them.

Evaluation: Have the student name 10 things that have use value for a large office building, or a school.

---

21. THE VALUE OF SCARCE GOODS

Purpose: To have students identify things that fulfill the idea of scarcity.

Meaning: The economic value of useful things depends upon their scarcity.

Procedure: Give students a list of goods and have them rank each item as to how scarce it is: Most scarce (1); Moderately scarce (2); Least scarce (3).

gravel	gold
silver	milk
coffee	uranium
wheat	Hawaiian pineapples
platinum	coal
gem diamonds	lumber

Value Questions For Discussion

1. Name some useful things that are most scarce.
2. Name some useful things that are not scarce.
3. How would you define scarcity?

Value Situation

Have the students identify an area of the world and give examples of useful things that are scarce in that area.

Evaluation: Have students list 5 useful things that are scarce in their community and 5 that are abundant.

---

22. THE VALUE OF REFINED AND PROCESSED GOODS

Purpose: To have the students identify useful things that exemplify the idea of refinement and processing.

Meaning: Useful things that are produced or provided with many refinements or much processing are generally scarcer than things that are not so refined or processed.

Procedure: Have the students place the following useful things in two categories—goods which have greater refinements (+), goods which have the least refinements (0).

Which Goods Involve More Refinement or Processing?

water piped to desert
water dipped from a stream
an apple
an apple pie
a hand-blown glass vase
a window-pane
a custom-made table
a mass-produced table
a handsaw
a factory with modern equipment

Value Questions For Discussion

1. If something involves more refining and processing, do you think it will be more available or less?
2. Do you think it will cost more or less?

Value Situation

Have the students name some of the refinements or processing of an article of clothing.

Evaluation: Have the students name 3 items that have a great number of processed qualities (refinements) and 3 items that have few such qualities.

---

23. IS IT EXPENSIVE?

Purpose: To have students identify goods and services that are economically valuable (expensive).

Meaning: The term "expensive" designates that which is economically valuable. The economic value of goods depends upon their scarcity. The scarcer a useful thing is, the greater its economic value (the higher the price).

50

Procedure: Place the following list on the chalkboard and have the students determine which items are "expensive."

a Rembrandt painting	a highly skilled physicist
a race horse	a racing car
waterfront property	an unskilled laborer
desert property	a rocket
an automobile factory	platinum

Value Questions For Discussion

1. Why is a Rembrandt economically valuable?
2. Why is desert property generally not expensive?
3. Can you think of an object that is economically valuable but that you might not want for your own use?
4. Name some services that are economically valuable.

Value Situations

Have the students do one or more of the following things.

1. Name some objects that were rare in the past but are no longer rare or expensive. (E.g.: books, spices, etc.)
2. List 2 or more consumer products that you would rank as *expensive* and 2 or more that are *inexpensive*.
3. Give reasons why the following items are expensive.
   gasoline
   medical services
   the space program

Value Statments

Have the students look up synonyms for *expensive* (e.g., *costly, high-priced, dear*), and find or write statements using them.

Evaluation: Have the students name 5 things that are economically valuable.

24. THE ECONOMIC VALUE OF SKILLS

Purpose: To have students identify skills that are economically valuable.

Meaning: Rare or highly developed skills are valuable economically (if there is great demand for them) and therefore yield the highest wages.

Procedure: The teacher may ask the students to consider which of the following people are the most highly skilled and would probably command the highest wages in the labor market.

airplane pilot	plumber
unskilled laborer	truck driver
computer programmer	mathematician
medical doctor	poet
registered nurse	sanitation worker
practical nurse	town council member
teacher	dentist
teacher's aide	dental assistant
auto mechanic	cellist
gas pump operator	TV star
crane operator	heavy-weight boxer
typist	professional football player
receptionist	chairman of the board

Value Questions For Discussion

1. Which occupations have high economic value on the labor market? Which have low economic value?
2. Can you think of jobs in the past which had high economic value?

Value Situation

The teacher may present the following question to the students for their written responses:

In selecting a career purely in terms of economic value, what careers would you be most likely to choose, and why?

Value Statements

Have the students prepare statements, based on the latest information, arguing that the following occupations will be economically valuable in the 1980s and explaining why.

computer specialist   oceanographer
space technician   major league pitcher
doctor

Evaluation: Have the students name 5 occupations that have high economic value.

Chapter 5

ETHICAL VALUE:
The Value of the Individual

Students can value themselves and others as ethical persons. This process involves the student in applying ethical concepts to himself and others.

An ethical person is one who fulfills his own unique definition of himself. The ethical person defines himself and fulfills that definition or self-concept. The person will be the more ethical the more he fulfills his concept of himself. A morally good person has integrity and self-respect. He is a self-actualizing person.

Ethical self-concepts are unique concepts. They define the self or the person as special, one-of-a-kind, as having personal identity and individuality. The person who does not fulfill or exemplify a unique self-concept will see himself only in his commonality—as commonplace, ordinary; as a type, an item like others of one sort or another; as a member of classes.

The ethical person chooses a self-concept or self-definition in the direction of the better or in the direction of improvement. A person cannot be morally good if his definition of himself is not in the direction of the "good."

There are three types of self-concepts that may be chosen—a practical self-concept, a principled self-concept, an intrinsic self-concept.

Students may choose themselves in a practical way. They may choose themselves psychologically as motivated persons. They may choose themselves socially as conforming to social role expectations. They may choose themselves economically as participating in the economic system.

Students may choose themselves in a principled way. They may choose to be guided by universally necessary principles such as the Golden Rule. Principles serve as a guide to action in instances where they apply.

Students may choose themselves in an intrinsic way. The intrinsic individual is in Kierkegaard's terms the "Knight of Faith." He is the person who chooses to have infinite involvement in the self and others—a sense of complete unity. He derives pure joy in relating to and being involved in the world around him. His characteristics are clarity, faith, trust, joy.

This section presents activities that will encourage students to develop the ability to value themselves and others as ethical persons. The activities are focused on choosing a self-definition, conforming to or fulfilling a self-definition, and improving a self-definition.

---

25. ETHICAL VALUE

Purpose: To have students identify instances of the fulfillment of their own singular definitions of themselves.

Meaning: Individuals may or may not conform to their concepts of themselves. *Honest* and *sincere* are some of the ethical terms used to describe a person who does conform to his concept of himself. *Dishonest* and *insincere* describe a person who does not conform to his concept. An ethical person is one who fulfills his own singular definition of himself (self-concept). An ethical person is one who is who and what he is and does not pretend to be who and what he is not. The ethical person is genuine, authentic.

Procedure: Have the students complete statements such as the following.

1. I am sincere when I _____ .
2. I am being true to myself when I _____ .
3. I am honest when I _____ .
4. I am genuine when I _____ .
5. I am real when I _____ .

6. I am forthright when I _____ .
7. I am dishonest when I _____ .
8. I am feigning when I _____ .
9. I am insincere when I _____ .
10. I am not true when I _____ .
11. I am a fake when I _____ .
12. I am not genuine when I _____ .
13. I speak with a forked tongue when I _____ .

Value Questions For Discussion

1. Do you actually conform to the idea you have of yourself? Give examples of when you do and when you do not.
2. How do you know when you are not conforming to your idea of yourself—when you are being insincere?
3. Do you know when you are acting in accordance with what you think of yourself (how you define yourself)?

Value Situations

Have the students participate in the following.

1. Write a diary entry for the period of a day. Indicate some words and actions that were true to yourself, or genuine, and some which were not.
2. Role-play an action that is not in conformity with who and what you are (your definition of yourself).

Evaluation: Have the students give one example of their acting in conformity with what they think of themselves and one that shows them not in conformity with their self-concepts.

---

26. NOT BEING MYSELF

Purpose: To have students identify instances of non-fulfillment of a person's self-concept.

Meaning: Sometimes individuals act in accordance with the expectations of others and are not being their own selves.

Procedure: Have students read the following statements describing persons who acted according to other people's expectations and not in accordance with their own self-concepts. Ask the students to tell how or why each person was not being true to himself or herself.

1. He takes care to laugh when he thinks a joke is not funny or looks bored when he is amused.
2. He is careful to applaud when he thinks a play is not good.
3. He dresses for the occasion yet is most uncomfortable.
4. She takes care to praise, even when she really thinks a person is unworthy.
5. At a formal dinner she remarks at the goodness of the cuisine while she can hardly finish the meal.
6. He criticizes a performance that he knows to be excellent.

Value Questions For Discussion

1. Tell about some times when you did not fulfill your self-concept—when you acted according to other people's expectations.
2. Tell about something showing that other people did not fulfill their self-concepts.

Value Situations

Ask students to participate in one or more of the following activities.

1. Role-playing: You are having your picture taken. Choose some inauthentic poses for yourself—poses that would show yourself not as you really are.
2. Using some of the following expressions, describe instances of not being one's own self.
   "playing possum"
   "wearing a mask"
   "following the crowd"
   "keep 'true self' in hiding"
   "I am only what other people regard me as being"
3. Select a character portrayed in literature who presented a "false front." Describe the character.

Evaluation: Have the students give 2 instances showing that they or someone else did not fulfill their self-concept but acted according to other people's expectations.

27. VALUING SELF-KNOWLEDGE

Purpose: To have students define and clarify their concepts of themselves.

Meaning: Every individual is unique. The more a unique individual differentiates himself—clarifies himself, sets himself forth, defines himself—the more ethical he is.

Procedure: Have the students indicate some things about themselves using the following categories.

My wishes	My feelings
My thoughts	My abilities
My words	My social relations
My tools	My relations with nature

Value Questions For Discussion

1. What is your idea about yourself?
2. Have you ever been wrong in your idea about yourself?
3. Do some people have clearer ideas about themselves than other people do?

Value Situation

Have the students tell about some things they have come to know about themselves in a crisis situation.

Evaluation: Have the students name two aspects of themselves that they are clear about.

---

28. ENHANCING THE ETHICAL SELF

Purpose: To have students be aware that they may increase their ethical self-development by increasing the ethical development of others.

Meaning: Improving the ethical development of others increases the ethical development of the self. Each person's moral or ethical life is part of the total human ethical life. To increase the moral life of a person is to help increase ethical life in general.

Procedure: Ask the students to tell how the following conduct enhances or improves others and thereby improves one's own ethical self.

> To help individuals have an opportunity to develop their highest potential.
> To see that others have a fair chance or equal opportunity.
> To be patient and tolerant with others.
> To stop cruelty and exploitation of others.
> To help bring about happiness.
> To help children grow into good adults.

Value Questions For Discussion
1. How does the above conduct enhance others?
2. Can you name some people who have helped your growth?

Value Situation
Have the students read about and report on outstanding persons who have enhanced the lives of others. Examples:
Helen Keller, Florence Nightingale

Evaluation: Have the students tell about a person who has enhanced the development of another.

---

29. DIMINISHING THE ETHICAL SELF

Purpose: To have the students become aware that the "ethical self" may be diminished by diminishing others.

Meaning: A self cannot fulfill itself by diminishing other selves.

Procedure: Have students tell how the following conduct diminishes others and therby oneself.

To be deceitful.

To be inconsiderate.

To be untruthful.

To be oppressive.

To be prejudiced.

To be wicked.

To be malicious.

To abuse others.

To ignore the rights
of others.

Value Questions For Discussion

1. How does the above conduct diminish or make less of others?
2. Can a person who conducts himself in those ways be morally good? Has that person chosen himself for the better?
3. How does a person become diminished when he hurts other persons?
4. Can a person enhance his ethical self by diminishing others?

Value Situation

Present the following ethical principle to the students and have them discuss the validity of the principle.

To limit a person's existence (growth) is to limit a part of the total of human existence and thereby to limit the existence of one's own self.

Evaluation: Give an instance of a person diminishing another person and thereby diminishing himself or herself.

---

30. VALUING SOCIAL EXPECTATIONS IN AN ETHICAL WAY

Purpose: To have the students give instances of their self-concepts being in conflict with social expectations.

Meaning: Very often social pressures are in conflict with a person's own self-concept. At times, in order to fulfill his or her own self-concept, a person must disregard social pressures.

Procedure: The teacher may ask students to read and respond to the following.

1. At times it pleases others when I am neat and tidy. Are there times when it doesn't suit me to be neat and tidy?

2. At times it pleases others when I sit quietly—when I am a "good boy" or "good girl." Is this always the best choice for me?
3. At times it pleases others when I am polite. Is this always the best choice for me in every situation?
4. At times it pleases others when I follow rules. Is this always the best choice for me?
5. At times it pleases others when I am forceful. Does this always suit me?

Value Questions For Discussion

1. Name some things that may please others but do not fit your idea of what is best for you.
2. Do you often have this conflict?

Value Situation

Have the students write about a situation in which there might be a conflict between what others demand of them and what they think is best for themselves.

Evaluation: Have the students give 2 instances of ways in which they feel their own understanding of what is best for them is in conflict with the demands of others.

---

31. CHOOSING A PRACTICAL SELF

Purpose: To have students identify instances of the fulfillment of a practical self-concept.

Meaning: Individuals may choose themselves in practical ways—as functioning in a social role, as functioning psychologically (having interests), as functioning in an economic system (in the labor market or as a consumer).

Procedure: The teacher may present to students the following statements about practical self-concepts chosen by individuals. Ask the students if any of these practical self-concepts are suited to them.

I am suited to being a parent.
It is my calling to be a doctor.
I was meant to be rich.
If I were not a teacher it would not be me.
It is my destiny to be a leader of men.
I want to satisfy my desires.
It is within me to be a musician.
It is an aspect of myself to be a student.

Value Questions For Discussion

1. Are the practical self-concepts you chose suited to you? Why?
2. Are there some practical self-concepts that are not suited to you?
3. Tell about a practical self-concept that you do fulfill.

Value Situations

Ask students to participate in one or more of the following.

1. Select a strong interest that is well suited to you. Write a short essay entitled "If I Didn't Like It I Wouldn't Be Me."
2. Interview some people and ask which social or vocational roles suit them and which do not. Ask if they feel they are really suited to a role they have chosen. (Ask questions like these: "What are you?" "Is that suited to you?" "Is it a part of yourself?" "What do you do about it?")
3. Role-play these value situations.
   a. When playing football you find it is not suited to you at all!
   b. You want to become a great pianist but find you hate to practice.
   c. You think of yourself as a budding writer, but can't think of a really interesting subject for an essay or poem.
   d. You are a mother or teacher, and find children very tiresome.

Evaluation: Have the students list one practical self-concept that is suited to them and one that is not.

32. CHOOSING A PRINCIPLED SELF-CONCEPT

Purpose: To have the students identify instances of the fulfillment of a principled self-concept.

Meaning: Individuals may choose themselves as principled individuals. To be principled is to choose a universal principle and to act in accordance with it. A principle is a logically necessary rule that holds in all circumstances to which it applies.

Procedure: The teacher may present to the students the universal principles listed below and have them tell if they or others have acted according to the principles.

1. "Act in such a way that you treat humanity, both in your own person and in the person of all others, never as a means only but always equally as an end." (Kant)
2. "If the consequences of A's doing x would be undesirable, then A ought not to do x." (Marcus G. Singer[1])
3. "We told these truths to be self-evident, that all Men are created equal, . . . " (Declaration of Independence)
4. "Do unto others as you would have them do unto you."

Value Questions For Discussion

1. When might it be appropriate for a person to act in accordance with one of the above principles?
2. Can you think of persons who always seem to act in accordance with a principle?

Value Situation

Present the following to the students:

The following persons might be viewed as having adhered to universal principles. What were the principles they chose and followed?

Gandhi, Martin Luther King, Joan of Arc, Lincoln, Jesus, Susan B. Anthony.

---

[1]"Moral Rules and Principles," in *Essays in Moral Philosophy*, A. I. Melden, ed. (University of Washington Press, 1958); cited from *Moral Education*, B. Chazan and G. Soltis, eds. (Teachers College Press, 1973), p. 106.

Value Statement

Have the students select a universal principle that might be suited to them and tell why it is suited to them.

Evaluation: Have the students name a historical figure who chose a principled self-concept.

---

33. ETHICAL "OUGHT"

Purpose: To have students recognize that individuals ought to choose themselves in the direction of improvement—in the direction of "what is better."

Meaning: Ethical "ought" indicates improvements to be made in self-development. Individuals ought to choose themselves in the direction of growth and improvement—in the direction of the better. Improvement always takes place in a context or a situation. "Ought" or "what is better" is always relative to the situation.

Procedure: Ask students to read the following selection from Martin Luther King's speech, "I Have A Dream."

I have a dream that one day this nation will rise up and live out the true meaning of its creed: . . . We hold these truths to be self-evident; that all men are created equal. I have a dream that one day on the red hills of Georgia the sons of former slaves and the sons of former slaveowners will be able to sit down together at the table of brotherhood. I have a dream that one day even the state of Mississippi, a desert state sweltering with the heat of injustice and oppression, will be transformed into an oasis of freedom and justice. And as we walk, we must make the pledge that we shall march ahead. We cannot turn back. . . . No, no we are not satisfied, and we will not be satisfied until justice rolls down like water and righteousness like a mighty stream. This is the faith with which I return to the South. With this faith we will be able to hew out of the mountain of despair a stone of hope. With this faith we will be able to transform the jangling discords of our nation into a beautiful symphony of brotherhood. With this faith we will be able to work together, to pray together, to stand up for freedom together, knowing that we will be free one day.

Value Questions For Discussion

1. What was Martin Luther King's chosen concept—what was his dream?
2. Was he committed to his dream?
3. Was his chosen self-concept in the direction of improvement for himself and for his people?
4. Did his actions indicate that he tried to fulfill his concept of himself as a leader of the black people in their fight for freedom and justice?

Evaluation: Have the students give a reason showing that Martin Luther King chose his self-concept in the direction of the better.

---

34. VALUING SELF-IMPROVEMENT

Purpose: To have students give examples of being in conformity with a self-concept that is in the direction of the better (improvement).

Meaning: A person's choice of self-concept is based on the idea of "ought." "Ought" means that a person should choose or prefer a self-concept that is "good," or in the direction of the better, and fulfill it.

Procedure: The teacher may have the students complete these statements.

1. At play I am the most I can be when I _____.
2. At home I am the best I can be when I _____.
3. At school I am all that I can be when I _____.
4. With others I am as good as I can be when I _____.
5. I am the least I can be when I _____.

Value Questions For Discussion

1. What are some ideas that you can have about yourself that are in the direction of the better (improvement)?
2. Can you fulfill your chosen ideas?

3. What are some ideas that you can have about yourself that are in the direction of the worse?

Evaluation: Have the students list one way they can improve in each of the following situations.
   a. as an athlete or other performer
   b. as a student
   c. as a friend

---

35. HOW DO YOU DEFINE YOURSELF?

Purpose: To have the students define aspects of their self-concept and determine whether they fulfill their chosen definition.

Meaning: Persons choose ideas about themselves. They may act in accordance with their ideas of themselves. At times they may not.

Procedure: Give students the following list and have them identify phrases that fit their ideas of themselves.

To be bossy	To be friendly
To be a bully	To be tough
To be clumsy	To be shy
To be careful	To be quiet
To collect things	To be generous
To be smart	To be talkative

Value Questions For Discussion

1. Do any of the above expressions depict you? Are there others that would better express your idea of yourself?
2. Do other people have the same idea about yourself as you do?
3. Do you act according to your idea of yourself?

Value Situation

Suggest that students do the following: Describe a situation in which you acted in a way that was inconsistent with your idea of yourself.

Evaluation: Have students give an instance of a literary character acting in accordance with his or her self ideal.

66

36. GOING AGAINST THE AUTHENTIC SELF

Purpose: To have students become aware of feelings of guilt or remorse they may have when they do not fulfill their own chosen self-
concept.

Meaning: The feeling of guilt can often be an indication that one is
violating one's basic sense of the self. People act in ways that violate
or are inconsistent with their basic selves, and they may then have
feelings of guilt or remorse.

Procedure: The teacher may ask students to tell or write about a time
when they did something they later felt sorry about.

Examples:

Hurting someone	Being cowardly
Being selfish	Acting stupidly
Being inconsiderate	Cheating
Not being truthful	Being unfair

Value Questions For Discussion

1. Name something you did which does not fit your sense of yourself
   —what you think you are.
2. Describe your reactions and feelings in that instance.

Value Situation

Have the students think of literary characters who acted in ways that
were basically against their self-concepts and then felt feelings of
guilt or remorse.

Examples:
"The Man Without a Country"
"Pinocchio"
"Lord Jim"

Evaluation: Have the students give an example of a person who did
not act in accordance with his conception of himself and who later
felt guilty or remorseful.

37. VALUING MOTIVES IN AN ETHICAL WAY

Purpose: To have students choose motives that are best suited to them—that are in the direction of improvement.

Meaning: Individuals can choose themselves as having interests and can select motives that are in the direction of the good.

Procedure: Have students complete the following sentences.

1. It is best for me to want _____.
2. It will improve me to like _____.
3. It is not good for me to like _____.
4. I love _____ but it is not good for me.
5. I am lucky to like _____ because it is good for me.
6. It would be better for me to like _____ rather than _____.
7. I always seem to want _____ when I shouldn't.
8. I would like to spend $50 on _____ when I should spend it on _____.
9. I ought to like _____.

Value Questions For Discussion

1. Are some motives better for you than others? What are things it is good for you to want?
2. What are some goals or desires that you ought to decide not to pursue?

Value Situation

Have students present an argument that something they want is good for them—is the direction of their improvement. Or they might argue that something they want is not good for them.

Evaluation: Ask students to identify 3 interests that would lead to their self-improvement.

38. VALUING ROLE EXPECTATIONS IN AN ETHICAL WAY

Purpose: To have students choose role expectations that are in the direction of improvement.

Meaning: Persons can choose themselves as conforming to role expectations that lead to self-improvement.

Procedure: The teacher may present the expectations indicated below and have the students select those that are best for them to conform to.

parents expect	school expects
friends expect	advertisers expect
troublemakers expect	the "gang" expects
doctor expects	salespersons expect
a bully expects	policemen expect

Value Questions For Discussion

1. Whose expectations are better for you to follow? Which are in the direction of improvement?
2. Which expectations are the worst for you to follow? Which would limit you?

Value Argument

Have the students present an argument that some expectations they have chosen to follow are in the direction of improvement.

Evaluation: Have the students select a role expectation they would not follow because it would not be best for them.

---

39. VALUING KNOWLEDGE IN AN ETHICAL WAY

Purpose: To have the students identify knowledge and skills that are in the direction of improvement for them.

Meaning: Persons can choose themselves as acquiring knowledge and skills that will lead to their self-improvement.

Procedure: The teacher may have the students identify the areas of knowledge that are best for them from among the following areas.

Mathematics

Science

Music

Parenting

Business

History

Art

Sports

Medicine

Homemaking

Economics

Engineering

Value Questions For Discussion

1. Are some types of knowledge better for you than others?
2. What types of knowledge and skills ought you to decide not to pursue?
3. In what ways would some knowledge areas not suit you and not lead to your development?

Value Dilemma

Suppose you have time to become involved with only one area of knowledge. Select that one area and give reasons for your choice.

Evaluation: Have the students identify one area of knowledge that suits them and will lead to their development. Then ask them to identify one area of knowledge that does not suit someone they know and will not lead to that person's development or improvement.

---

40. VALUING CONSUMPTION IN AN ETHICAL WAY

Purpose: To have students identify consumer goods and services that are in the direction of personal improvement.

Meaning: Individuals can choose consumer goods and services that lead to personal improvement.

Procedure: Have the students use the general categories listed below to give specific examples of goods and services that are personally suited to them—that would lead to their personal improvement.

Clothes	Housing
Tools	Vacations
Food	Education
Health care	Art
Transportation	Music

Value Questions For Discussion

1. What types of goods and services are personally suited to you and would lead to your improvement? Why do some goods suit you more than others?
2. Name some goods and services that are not suited to you and would not lead to your improvement.

Value Situation

Have the students list three consumer items that might suit their lifestyle as students.

Evaluation: Have the students describe two personal choices involving buying goods and services that suit them as opposed to those that do not suit them.

---

41. CARING FOR THE IMPROVEMENT OF THE WORLD

Purpose: To have the students view or choose themselves as persons who care for the world around them.

Meaning: One of the important ethical "oughts" is that ethical persons are concerned with and committed to the improvement of the world around them. Individuals may feel a sense of well-being as the world fulfills itself and gets better. The improvement of the world becomes associated with the improvement of the self.

Procedure: Ask the students to tell or write about which aspects of the world they would commit themselves to improve. Each student might choose one of the following areas and show how he or she might contribute to improvement in that area.

Education
Health
Environment
Urban life
Economics

Value Questions For Discussion

1. How do you react when things in the world that you are concerned with are diminished or destroyed?
2. How do you react when things in the world are improved?

Value Situation

Have the students tell how the following persons committed themselves to the improvement of an aspect of the world.

Louis Pasteur
Jonas Salk
Woodrow Wilson

Value Argument

Have the students take the position that things in their community ought to be improved and that it is part of their responsibility to see to it.

Evaluation: Have the students identify two areas in their community that ought to be improved and ask for their suggestions for improvement.

Chapter 6

SOCIAL-ETHICAL VALUE:
Citizenship and Group
Participation

Students can value groups of persons by applying social-ethical concepts. Important social-ethical concepts are group involvement, group identity, and group decision-making. In performing social-ethical valuation, students establish a social-ethical concept such as group involvement and judge groups of persons to determine if they exemplify the concept.

A group may or may not establish and fulfill its own unique definition. A group or institution will be more socially ethical the more it fulfills its own decided-upon goals and norms.

A group may decide upon a definition that is in the direction of the better—in the direction of improvement. A group cannot be "good" from a social-ethical point of view if its definition is not in the direction of the good.

Words and phrases such as *freedom, democracy, autonomy, independence, solidarity, group involvement*, and *citizenship* refer to the social-ethical "good." Terms such as *dependent, controlled, divided*, and *lack of group involvement* refer to lack of social-ethical value.

This chapter presents activities that will encourage students to value themselves and others as group members. Students will be encouraged to view themselves as "citizens," participating in and involved with local, regional, and national groups. Instructional activities will assist students in becoming aware of critical group processes such as decision-making and goal-setting.

72

42. THE SOCIAL-ETHICAL GROUP

Purpose: The purpose of this activity is to have students identify groups which fulfill their own group definition.

Meaning: Social-ethical groups are groups which have their own symbols, institutions, and goals. Political and social-ethical terms such as *freedom, independence, decision-making, self-directing,* and so on may be used to describe a group that conforms to its own goals, institutions, and symbols. Terms such as *oppression* or *tyranny* may be used to describe a group which does not conform to its own goals, institutions, and norms.

Procedure: The teacher may have the students complete the following statements with the names of appropriate groups.

1. We, the _____ are self-governing.
2. We, the _____ were oppressed.
3. We, the _____ were colonized.
4. We, the _____ were trampled down.
5. We, the _____ fought for our freedom.
6. We, the _____ have group autonomy.
7. We, the _____ lived under tyranny.
8. We, the _____ have free political choice.

Value Questions For Discussion

1. Name some groups that are free—self-defining (self-choosing).
2. Name some groups that are oppressed and not self-choosing—not free.

Value Situation

Have the students tell or write about a group that is free—a group that has defined its own goals, symbols, and institutions (rules) and conforms to them.

Evaluation: Have the students name two groups that are free and two that are oppressed.

43. INVOLVEMENT WITH GROUP GOALS AND NORMS

Purpose: To have students identify groups that fulfill their own group definition.

Meaning: Social-ethical groups define and are involved with their own goals, symbols, and norms.

Procedure: The teacher may have students complete a chart that lists (*a*) Group Norms or Rules, (*b*) Group Goals, and (*c*) Group Symbols, for each of these groups:

The New York Times	The Knights of the Round Table
The Ford Motor Co.	The Pony Express
The First Continental Congress	The Boston Symphony Orchestra
Columbia University	The Lewis and Clark expedition

Value Questions For Discussion

1. What are some of the defined goals, symbols, and norms of the above groups?
2. Are the above groups self-directing? In what ways?

Value Situation

Have the students write a specific goal that a group they are familiar with has established.

Evaluation: Have the students select a group and establish some goals, symbols, and norms.

---

44. "WE THE PEOPLE..."

Purpose: To have the students view the American nation as a group striving for independence and fulfilling its group definition.

Meaning: The founders of the American nation presented value arguments defending their decision to fight for independence. Aspects of these arguments are presented in the Declaration of Independence.

Procedure: Have the students read the following selections from the Declaration of Independence.

We hold these truths to be self-evident, that all Men are created equal, that they are endowed by their Creator with certain unalienable Rights, that among these are Life, Liberty, and the pursuit of Happiness, — That to secure these Rights, Governments are instituted among Men, deriving their just powers from the consent of the governed, — that whenever any Form of Government becomes destructive of these ends, it is the Right of the People to alter or to abolish it, and to institute new Government, laying its foundation on such principles and organizing its powers in such form, as to them shall seem most likely to effect their Safety and Happiness. Prudence, indeed, will dictate that Governments long established should not be changed for light and transient causes; . . . But when a long train of abuses and usurpations, pursuing invariably the same Object, evinces a design to reduce them under absolute Despotism, it is their right, it is their duty, to throw off such Government, and to provide new Guards for their future security. — Such has been the patient sufferance of these Colonies; and such is now the necessity which constrains them to alter their former Systems of Government. The history of the present King of Great Britain is a history of repeated injuries and usurpations, all having in direct object the establishment of an absolute Tyranny over these States. To prove this, let Facts be submitted to a candid World. —

He has refused his Assent to Laws, the most wholesome and necessary for the public good.— . . .

He has combined with others to subject us to a jurisdiction foreign to our constitution, and unacknowledged by our laws; giving his Assent to their Acts of pretended Legislation:— . . .

For cutting off our Trade with all Parts of the world:—

For imposing Taxes on us without our Consent:—

For depriving us, in many cases, of the benefits of Trial by Jury:—

For transporting us beyond Seas to be tried for pretended offences:— . . .

For taking away our Charters, abolishing our most valuable Laws, and altering fundamentally the Forms of our Governments:— . . .

In every stage of these Oppressions We have Petitioned for Redress in the most humble terms: Our repeated Petitions have been answered only by repeated injury. . . . We, therefore, the Representatives of the United States of America, in General Congress, Assembled, appealing to the Supreme Judge of the world for the rectitude of our intentions, do in the Name and by Authority of the good People of these Colonies, solemnly publish and declare, That these United Colonies are, and of Right ought to be, Free and

Independent States; that they are Absolved from all Allegiance to the
British Crown, and that all political connection between them and the State
of Great Britain, is and ought to be totally dissolved; and that as Free and
Independent States, they have a full Power to levy War, conclude Peace,
contract Alliances, establish Commerce, and to do all other Acts and Things
which Independent States may of right do.—And for the support of this
Declaration, with a firm reliance on the protection of divine Providence,
we mutually pledge to each other our Lives, our Fortunes, and our sacred
Honor.

Value Questions For Discussion

1. According to the Declaration of Independence, under what con-
   ditions are a group of people justified in establishing their own
   independent government?
2. In what ways did the writers of the Declaration feel they lacked
   independence?
3. How did they state their determination to establish a free and independent government?
4. How was American independence finally won?

Value Situation

Have the students research some other nations that have become independent and read their justifications for gaining independence.

Evaluation: Have the students give one argument justifying the Colonies' struggle for independence from England.

---

45. POLITICAL "OUGHT"

Purpose: To have students identify instances of non-fulfillment of
group definition and to suggest ways of improving group definition.

Meaning: Political or social-ethical "ought" indicates non-fulfillment
of group definition. Political "ought" indicates improvements that
need to be made in the fulfillment of group definition.

Procedure: The teacher may give the students the following direc-
tions.

As citizens of the United States we ought to choose goals that would improve the country. Goals in the areas of health, education, housing, national economy, equal opportunity, energy, and ecology are not clearly defined and are in the process of being defined. Suggest some specific goals for the United States in those areas. Use the following criteria to consider the goals you suggest: (*a*) Are the goals consistent with other aspects of the country's self-definition? (*b*) Are the goals in the direction of improvement?

Value Questions For Discussion

1. Where is the American nation lacking in the definition of some of its goals?
2. What are some goals you can suggest to improve the American nation?

Value Situation

Have the students find some past decisions made by the American nation that were in the direction of improvement and some decisions that were not in the direction of improvement.

Evaluation: Have the students describe a goal which the American nation ought to include in its group definition—a goal that would be in the direction of improvement.

---

46. THE VALUE OF GROUP CO-OPERATION

Purpose: To have students view different types of groups as exemplifying unity, co-operation, and group identity.

Meaning: Groups may be viewed as co-operative unities.

Procedure: Read the following story to the students.

An old man called his seven sons to him. He gave his oldest son a bundle of seven sticks to break. The son tried and tried but he could not break the bundle of sticks. Each of the sons in turn tried to break it. Each son failed. The old man then untied the bundle of sticks and gave one to each son. Each son broke his stick easily. The old man asked them what they thought this meant.

Value Questions For Discussion

1. Why does the father, in the account described, think that unity is important?
2. Name some groups in which there is co-operation and unity.

Value Situations

1. Have the students find in magazines pictures that show (a) co-operation in the family, (b) co-operation in a community.
2. Students may select a symbol of a group and tell how the symbol represents the unity of the group.
3. Students may write an account of a group that is united, using some of the following synonyms: "pulling together," "getting along with others," "on the same team."

Evaluation: Have the students list 3 actions showing that a group is working together and 3 showing a group is not working together.

---

47. "WE ARE A FAMILY"

Purpose: To have the students view the "family" as exemplifying a unified group.

Meaning: Group members become conscious of their membership in groups. They become aware of decision-making processes, group norms, group symbols, and group goals.

Procedure: The teacher may ask the students to participate in one or more of the following activities.

1. Names identify unique family groups. Trace your family name.
2. Construct a family tree showing the members of your unique family group.

3. In the Middle Ages, families designed their own crests—family emblems—to identify a particular family. Design an emblem for your family that represents the unique character of your family.
4. List some objects that are special for your family—mementos, souvenirs, and so on.
5. List some of the particular rules that your family abides by that make your family different from other families.
6. List some family actions that correspond to the norms and goals chosen by your family.
7. List some family actions that may not correspond to the norms and goals chosen by your family.

Value Questions For Discussion

1. What are some important symbols, norms, and goals of your family?
2. What are some important symbols, norms, and goals of other families you know?

Value Situations

Have the students participate in the following activities.

1. Name some things that make the following families unique. The Rockefellers, the Kennedys, the Adamses.
2. Select a biography of a family and determine whether the family chose itself the best way it could, given the circumstances.

Value Argument

Have the students identify a situation in which they think their family acted as a unit in the best way possible.

Evaluation: Have the students list one family symbol and 3 family rules.

48. THE VALUE OF FAMILY UNITY

Purpose: To have the students view the "family" as exemplifying a unified group.

Meaning: Groups may be viewed as entities, unities which fulfill their own symbols, roles, norms, goals. The family gorup may be valued or shown in this way.

Procedure: The teacher may present the following categories to students and have them list for each category things that belong to their family.

Family name	Family traditions and rituals
Family home	Family talents
Persons in family	Family activities
Family friends	Family memorabilia
Family rules	

Value Questions For Discussion

1. What are some specific things that show that your family is united? What are some family traditions, rules, etc.?
2. Do you think your family has defined itself in the best way it could?
3. Can you think of ways of improving your family's group definition?

Value Situation

Have the students select a family group—from literature or television—and describe how the family defines itself.

Evaluation: Have the students list three family goals and three family rules that contribute to the integration of the family.

Chapter 7

ESTHETIC VALUE:
Beauty

Students can value things esthetically—as beautiful. In this process the student applies esthetic concepts to things. An important esthetic concept is the uniqueness of things. Esthetic valuation is viewing things in a unique way. In performing esthetic valuation, students establish an esthetic concept such as uniqueness and determine the way in which things exemplify that concept.

Things will be the more esthetically valuable the more they fulfill their unique concept. Words and phrases such as *beauty, novelty, a fresh look, viewing in a special way, an imaginative view,* and *an unfettered look* express the esthetic "good." Terms such as *ordinary, ugly, commonplace,* and *sameness* indicate absence of esthetic value.

Esthetic value develops from the application of esthetic theories to individual things. Applications of such theories as those of Susanne Langer are the basis of esthetic value.

This chapter presents activities that will help students to value things esthetically—as "beautiful." Students will be encouraged to be aware of what things seem unique or beautiful to them, and also to take common, ordinary, everyday items and look at them in an imaginative and creative way.

49. "THAT'S BEAUTIFUL!"

Purpose: To have students identify instances of things fulfilling the idea of uniqueness.

Meaning: Esthetic value is the value of things perceived as unique or special—including ordinary objects viewed in an imaginative, novel, or creative way. *Beautiful* is an esthetic interpretation of the basic value term *good*. *Mediocrity, monstrosity,* and *ugliness* are some words that indicate esthetic worthlessness.

Procedure: Have the students identify some things they view in an esthetic way—as beautiful— and also some things they think are esthetically worthless.

I find great enjoyment in listening to _____.
I saw _____ in a novel way.
I took an imaginative view of _____.
I took a fresh look at _____.
My enjoyment of looking at _____ is of great value to me.
I feel that _____ (a musical composition) is a masterpiece.
I thought _____ was a beautiful moment.
I found _____ to be a gourmet dish.
Suddenly _____ looked different and special to me.
After seeing the picture of it, I saw _____ as beautiful.
_____ is a beautiful flower.
I view _____ in a special way.
I think _____ (a musical composition) is just noise.
The _____ (a building) is a monstrosity.
I consider _____ (a play) to be a flop.
_____ (type of fashion) is a rag.
_____ is not beautiful.
_____ in the environment is ugly.

Value Questions For Discussion

1. What are some things you view as unique or beautiful?
2. What are some things you find lacking in esthetic value or beauty?
3. Should everyone agree about what is beautiful?
4. What kinds of feelings do you have when something seems very special or beautiful to you?

Value Statement

Have the students write an account describing the esthetic experience they had when they saw an object in an imaginative way.

Value Situation

The following are some things that are often portrayed in various art forms. Have each student find or create an esthetic depiction of one of these things:

a rainbow	a sand dune	a river
an ocean wave	a tree	a cloud

Evaluation: Have the students name something they view in an esthetic way—as having uniqueness—and describe the esthetic experience (their involvement with the thing).

---

50. VALUING A SNACK IN A UNIQUE WAY

Purpose: To have students view an ordinary thing as fulfilling a unique concept.

Meaning: An ordinary thing may be viewed in an esthetic way. In this case, the thing (a snack) is given various novel associations through poetic, metaphorical treatment.

Procedure: Ask the students to read the following passage by Thomas Wolfe, expressing a special and unique view of "A snack!"[1]

What shall it be now? What shall it be? A snack! A snack! . . .

I think—now let me see—h'm now!—well, perhaps I'll have a slice or two of that pink Austrian ham that smells so sweet and pungent and looks so pretty and so delicate there in the crisp garlands of the parsley leaf!—and yes, perhaps, I'll have a slice of this roast beef, as well—h'm now!—yes, I think that's what I'm going to do—say a slice of red rare meat there at the centre—ah-h! There you are! yes, that's the stuff, that does quite nicely, thank you—with just a trifle of that crisp bacon crackling there to oil the lips and make its passage easy, and a little of that cold but brown and oh most—brawny gravy—and, yes, sir!—I think I *will*, now, that it occurs to me a slice of that plump chicken—some white meat, thank you, at the breast—ah, there it is!—how sweetly doth the noble fowl submit to the swift and keen persuasion of the knife—and now perhaps, just for our diet's healthy balance, a spoonful of those lima beans, as gay as April and as sweet as butter, a tomato slice or two, a speared forkful of those thin sliced cucumbers—ah! what a delicate and toothsome pickle they do make—what sorcerer invented them—a little corn perhaps, a bottle of this milk, a pint of butter and that crusty loaf of bread—and even this moon-haunted wilderness were paradise enow—with just a snack—a snack—a snack!

Value Questions For Discussion

1. In what ways is this depiction of a snack not ordinary?
2. How does the author express the *extra*ordinary?
3. Is this a creative and imaginative way to look at a snack?

Value Situation

Have students find pictures or verbal depictions that make ordinary things seem special, unique, or beautiful.

Evaluation: Have the students write a poem or paragraph depicting an ordinary thing in a unique way.

---

[1] Thomas Wolfe, *Of Time and the River* (1935), pp. 542-43. Used by permission of Charles Scribner's Sons, New York, and William Heinemann Ltd, London.

Chapter 8

POETIC AND LITERARY VALUE:
Words as Metaphors

Students can value words poetically, by applying poetic concepts. An important poetic concept is the uniqueness of words used in or as metaphors. Poetic valuation is viewing words in a unique way. Students establish a poetic concept such as metaphor and determine how words or sets of words represent metaphors or sets of metaphors.

Words have poetic value when they fulfill the concept of metaphor. "The fog comes on little cat feet" is a poetic metaphor. Terms such as *poetic*, *metaphorical*, and *literary* refer to language that is valuable poetically. *Analytic* and *expository* describe language relatively lacking in poetic value.

Poetic value develops from the application of theories of literary criticism and linguistics. The concept of metaphor is central to literary theory, and when applied to words it produces poetic valuing.

This chapter presents activities that will help students value words poetically through appreciation of metaphors. The activities will also encourage students to create their own metaphors to depict things in special ways.

51. POETIC VALUE

Purpose: To have students identify words used so as to exemplify the concept of metaphor.

Meaning: Poetic value is words viewed uniquely, imaginatively. The metaphor depicts an ordinary thing in an extraordinary way, through analogy. From sets of metaphors emerges poetic value.

Procedure: Have the students read the following poem by John Masefield.

SEA FEVER[1]

I must go down to the seas again, to the
    lonely sea and the sky,
And all I ask is a tall ship and a star
    to steer her by,
And the wheel's kick and the wind's song
    and the white sail's shaking,
And a gray mist on the sea's face, and a
    gray dawn breaking.

I must go down to the seas again, for the
    call of the running tide
Is a wild call and a clear call that may
    not be denied;
And all I ask is a windy day with the
    white clouds flying,
And the flung spray and the blown spume,
    and the seagulls crying.

I must go down to the seas again, to the
    vagrant gipsy life,
To the gull's way and the whale's way where
    the wind's like a whetted knife;
And all I ask is a merry yarn from a laughing
    fellow-rover,
And quiet sleep and a sweet dream when the
    long trick's over.

---

[1]From *Poems: Complete Edition*, by John Masefield (1953). Used by permission of the Macmillan Company, New York, and The Society of Authors, London.

Value Questions For Discussion

1. What metaphors did the poet create? Name some.
2. What is the total impression given by the metaphors?
3. Do you think of the sea the way the metaphors in the poem depict it?

Evaluation: Have the students attempt to create some metaphors—of the sea or something else.

---

52. THE VALUE OF METAPHOR

Purpose: To have students identify words that exemplify the concept of metaphor.

Meaning: Poetic value is words viewed uniquely, imaginatively. The metaphor depicts an ordinary thing in an extraordinary way through analogy. From sets of metaphors emerges poetic value.

Procedure: Ask students to list the descriptive or expositional properties of "fog." Examples:

A vapor condensed to fine particles of water suspended in the lower atmosphere.
Differs from a cloud in being near the ground.
Distinguished from mist in being less transparent.
Thick condition of the atmosphere.
Murky.

Then have the students read the following poem by Carl Sandburg:

FOG[2]
The fog comes
    on little cat feet.
It sits looking
    over harbor and city
    on silent haunches
    and then moves on.

---

[2]From *Chicago Poems* by Carl Sandburg, copyright 1916 by Holt, Rinehart and Winston, Inc.; copyright 1944 by Carl Sandburg. Reprinted by permission of Harcourt Brace Jovanovich, Inc.

Value Questions For Discussion

1. Is the poem metaphorical? Identify the metaphors.
2. What does a metaphor do? How does it make an analogy?
3. How does a metaphor show the unique or the particular?
4. How does the metaphor in the poem give unity to the idea of fog?
5. How does the metaphor seem to shape the notion of fog and give it singularity and the special quality of a thing-in-itself?
6. How do the descriptive statements show the common or class characteristics of fog?

Value Situation

Have the students select an ordinary thing (such as a tree) and create a metaphor which will give an impression of the thing being unique and special in itself and not viewed as a member of a class.

Evaluation: Have the students select a poem and identify the central metaphors of the poem.

---

53. VALUING "CHICAGO" METAPHORICALLY

Purpose: To have students identify words that exemplify the concept of metaphor.

Meaning: Poetic value may be depicted by a set of metaphors (a poem).

Procedure: Have the students read the following poem by Carl Sandburg:

CHICAGO[3]

Hog-Butcher for the world,
Tool-maker, Stacker of Wheat,
Player with Railroads and the Nation's Freight-handler;
Stormy, husky, brawling.

---

[3]From *Chicago Poems* by Carl Sandburg, copyright 1916 by Holt, Rinehart and Winston, Inc., copyright 1944 by Carl Sandburg. Reprinted by permission of Harcourt Brace Jovanovich, Inc.

City of the Big Shoulders:
They tell me you are wicked and I believe them, for I have seen your
   painted women under the gas lamps luring the farm boys.
And they tell me you are crooked, and I answer; Yes, it is true I have
   seen the gunman kill and go free to kill again.
And they tell me you are brutal and my reply is: On the faces of
   women and children I have seen the marks of wanton hunger.
And having answered so I turn once more to those who sneer at this
   my city, and I give them back the sneer and say to them:
Come and show me another city with lifted head singing so proud to
   be alive and coarse and strong and cunning.
Flinging magnetic curses amid the toil of piling job on job, here is a
   tall bold slugger set vivid against the little soft cities;
Fierce as a dog with tongue lapping for action, cunning as a savage
   pitted against the wilderness,
   Bareheaded,
   Shoveling,
   Wrecking,
   Planning,
   Building, breaking, rebuilding,
Under the smoke, dust all over his mouth, laughing with white teeth,
Under the terrible burden of destiny laughing as a young man
   laughs,
Laughing even as an ignorant fighter laughs who has never lost a
   battle,
Bragging and laughing that under his wrist is the pulse, and under
   his ribs the heart of the people.
   Laughing!
Laughing the stormy, husky, brawling laughter of youth; half-na-
   ked, sweating, proud to be Hog-Butcher, Tool-maker, Stacker of
   Wheat, Player with Railroads, and Freight-handler to the Nation.

Value Questions For Discussion

1. How does the poem depict Chicago?
2. How does the poet use particular images to give the total impression of raw power?
3. Does the poem give you that impression?

Evaluation: Have the students point out one or more phrases representing the poem's central metaphor (depicting the kind of thing or person the city reminds one of).

Chapter 9

TECHNOLOGICAL VALUE:
Machines and Engineering

Students can value things in terms of technology, by applying concepts such as structure and system. In performing technological valuation, students establish a technological concept (e.g., mechanical system) and judge things to determine the way in which they exemplify the concept.

Machine, mechanical, engineered are terms that represent the "good" of technological value—that which is technologically valuable. *Malfunction, inoperative, junk* refer to what is technologically faulty.

Technological value develops from applications of physical science, as in technology and engineering. Technical theories such as those of Thomas Edison are the basis of technological value.

This chapter presents activities that will encourage students to view the world from the technological perspective: to value machines and other structures whose parts are systematically interrelated, and to become aware of the structure, organization, and systematic qualities of such things.

54. THE VALUE OF TECHNOLOGY

Purpose: To have students identify things that have technological value.

Meaning: A mechanical thing may be valued as a system with its parts in structured and systematic relation. That which is valuable technologically is engineered and is operative.

Procedure: Have the students complete these statements:

1. _____ is well engineered.
2. _____ is accurate.
3. The parts of _____ go together.
4. _____ has precision.
5. _____ is mechanical.
6. _____ operates.
7. _____ is not precise.
8. _____ does not work as it should.
9. _____ is inaccurate.
10. _____ does not operate.
11. _____ is malfunctioning.
12. _____ is junk.
13. _____ used to work well but is now broken down.

Value Questions For Discussion

1. Name some things that are engineered, organized, precise, and have interrelated parts which operate.
2. Name some things which lack precision and system and which are poorly engineered. (E.g., some toys and small appliances.)

Value Situations

Have the students participate in one of the following activities.
1. Name some types of technologies used in the following areas:
    space
    aeronautics
    medicine
    oceanography
    meteorology

2. Study and report on technologies involved in the invention of one of the following:
   steam engine
   radio
   airplane

Evaluation: Have the students name two things that are well engineered or structured and have technological value.

---

55. TECHNOLOGICAL "OUGHT"

Purpose: To have students identify some lackings in technological performance and suggest ways of improving technological performance.

Meaning: Technological "ought" indicates a lacking in technological performance — improvements that need to be made.

Procedure: The teacher may have the students list some technological improvements that ought to be made in one or more of the following areas.

Medicine	Planes
Space	Cars
Energy	Railroads

Value Questions For Discussion

1. What technologies would improve the above areas?
2. What ought to be done in terms of technological improvements?

Value Situation

Have students study and report on how one of the following persons improved technology:

Archimedes	Marie Curie
Robert Fulton	Guglielmo Marconi
Benjamin Franklin	Wernher von Braun
Thomas Edison	

Evaluation: Have the students identify a technological lack in an area and suggest a technological improvement.

Chapter 10

LEGAL VALUE:
The Value of the Law

Students can view persons or groups of persons legally, by applying legal concepts. Legal concepts are concepts formulated for structuring and ordering interpersonal or institutional relations. In performing legal valuation, students establish legal concepts and judge interacting persons to determine whether they conform to the concepts.

Words such as *lawful, law-abiding,* and *constitutional* are often used to refer to legal values; *illegal* and *criminal* refer to nonconformance with legal concepts.

This chapter presents activities that will encourage students to value interacting persons as conforming to or not conforming to the law—and to view laws and regulations as means of controlling or systematizing interpersonal relationships.

56. THE LAW

Purpose: To have students identify social acts that conform to the law.

Meaning: Interpersonal relations may be valued as structured and formally ordered. Terms such as *legal, constitutional, lawful* express that which is legally "good."

Procedure: Have students complete the following value statements.

1. _____ is unconstitutional.
2. _____ was a lawless breed.
3. _____ is legal.
4. _____ is illegal.
5. _____ is a constitutional guarantee.
6. _____ is a crime in this state.
7. _____ is a driving violation.
8. _____ is against the law.

Value Questions For Discussion

1. Name some acts that are legal—acts which conform to the law.
2. Name some acts that are illegal—acts which do not conform to the law.

Value Situation

Have the students name five rights guaranteed by the constitution.

Evaluation: Have the students describe an illegal act.

---

57. LEGAL INTERACTIONS

Purpose: To have students give instances of persons conforming to the law.

Meaning: Persons or groups can be judged in terms of defined interpersonal relationships. Legal value views interpersonal relationships as formally structured, ordered, precise. Groups of persons may be viewed as conforming to these legal definitions or not conforming to them.

Procedure: Present to the students the following legal definitions concerning the leasing of apartments.

1. Parties: This lease made the 14th day of March, 1977, between ESI Enterprises and John Stewart and Ann Stewart.
2. Premises: The landlord hereby leases to the tenant, and the tenant hereby hires and takes from the landlord, the apartment known as 2Q on the 2nd floor in the building known as Riveredge at 1 Park Place, Hastings, New York.
3. Term: The apartment is to be used and occupied solely as a private dwelling apartment, by the tenant and the family of the tenant, consisting of 3 persons, for a term to commence on the 1st day of May, 1977, and to end the 30th day of April, 1979.
4. Rent: The annual rent of $2,400.00 is due and payable in equal monthly installments of $200.00, each on the first day of each and every month during the term.
5. Improvements: All improvements, additions and alterations made by the tenant to or upon the premises, shall be attached to the premises, and become the property of the landlord.
6. Services: The landlord will furnish the following services in the building: (a) hot and cold water in reasonable quantities, (b) steam heat during the cold season in each year, (c) passenger elevator service.

The teacher may then have students devise illustrative cases in which (a) a tenant is not in conformity with the above terms of the lease, and (b) a landlord is not in conformity with the terms.

Value Questions For Discussion

1. How might a tenant not be in conformity with the terms of the lease?
2. How might a landlord not be in conformity with the terms of the lease?

Evaluation: Have the students state a law that they know and show how persons may or may not be in conformity with the law.

PART III

Activities Interrelating the Value Realms and Dimensions

Chapter 11

THE VALUE REALMS:
Alternative Value
Perspectives

Having a system or typology of values allows students to view phenomena from different significant perspectives. Students can value things from the alternative perspectives of the various value realms.

This kind of valuing involves judging a phenomenon to determine whether or how it exemplifies or fulfills alternative conceptual frameworks. A positive value is to view the world from alternative conceptual frameworks—to be able to apply various kinds of value criteria to phenomena. To have only a limited view is disvalue. To be value blind in some of the value areas is to see the world from only a limited perspective.

This chapter presents activities that will encourage students to value the world from the alternative perspectives of the value realms: ethical, social-ethical, economic, psychological, social, esthetic, legal. Instructional activities will assist students to become aware of multiple value perspectives, to become aware of the possibilities of viewing the same thing from alternative value perspectives, to select value perspectives that are appropriate to the situation, to set priorities among the value realms, and to recognize and use the language of the various value realms.

58. ALTERNATIVE VALUE PERSPECTIVES

Purpose: To have students identify instances of the fulfillment of multiple value perspectives.

Meaning: Individuals may value from the perspective of different value realms.

Procedure: The teacher may have the students write answers to the following questions.

I. *People can value themselves socially in social roles:*
How well do I perform my roles as a family member? Student? Friend? Neighbor?

II. *I can value myself ethically—in being what I am:*
Have I chosen or defined myself?
Do other people determine what I am?
Have I chosen myself in the direction of improvement?
What are my commitments?
Do I conform to my definition of myself?

III. *I can value myself psychologically:*
What are some of my motivations?
What are the things I am most interested in?
What are some short-term motivations that I have?
What are some long-term motivations that I have?
What are some of my motivations that are most useful to me?

IV. *I can value myself in terms of my value on the labor market in an economic way:*
Approximately what salary could I command now for the kinds of jobs I can do?
What salary range would I be able to command in the future, with enhanced skills and more education?

V. *I can value myself as a legal entity—as abiding by the law:*
What are my legal rights under the Constitution?
What are some state laws that apply to me?
What are some community laws that apply to me?
What are some work laws that apply to me?

Value Questions For Discussion

1. How is valuing people economically different from valuing people psychologically or ethically?
2. How is valuing myself psychologically different from valuing myself ethically?

Evaluation: Have the students describe instances of valuing themselves psychologically, economically, and ethically.

---

59. LANGUAGE AND THE VALUE REALMS

Purpose: To have students use appropriate language to express the values of the different realms.

Meaning: Various expressions may be used to identify values of the different value realms.

Procedure: The teacher may have the students categorize the value statements listed below on a chart according to the type of value expressed.

I like to travel.
That is a costly item.
I do what is expected of me.
I am my own person.
I try to be honest.
I derive great enjoyment from the music of Brahms.
I delight in being who and what I am.
He does not pretend to be anything he is not.
The system is operating.
The artist has a fresh way of looking at it.
He caught a glimpse of the uniqueness of the object.

Value Situation

Have the students participate in the following activities.

1. Role-playing: One person valuing a thing from an economic point of view and another person valuing the same thing from an esthetic point of view.

2. The following persons often make statements about various value areas. Write short accounts using value statements that persons in these roles might make.

an economist

a psychologist   a sociologist

an art critic   an engineer

Value Questions For Discussion

1. What are some ethical value statements?
2. Give some statements for some of the other value areas.

Evaluation: Have the students use statements to express an economic value, a social value, and a psychological value.

---

60. VALUING FROM DIFFERENT PERSPECTIVES

Purpose: To have students identify instances of the fulfillment of multiple value perspectives.

Meaning: Phenomena may be valued from the various perspectives of the value realms.

Procedure: The teacher may ask students to participate in the following.

Let us value Western Airlines from different perspectives.

Tell how each of the persons described here might value the airline according to his or her particular perspective.

1. A financial expert who is concerned with economic aspects of the company.
2. A mechanical engineer concerned with how the planes operate.
3. An advertiser who is concerned with motivating people to fly.
4. A passenger concerned with getting good service.
5. A personnel supervisor who expects airline employees to fulfill job requirements.

Value Questions For Discussion

1. Do economic principles apply to airlines?

2. Does technological value apply to airlines?
3. Do social expectations apply?
4. Do you know of any airlines whose equipment may not be me-chanically safe, or any that are in financial trouble, or any that do not give good service?

Value Situation

Have the students value the following from different perspectives: (*a*) a commuter railroad; (*b*) a department store; (*c*) an ocean liner.

Evaluation: Have the students show how different value perspectives apply to an automobile.

---

61. LANGUAGE EXPRESSING DIFFERENT VALUES

Purpose: To have students use language appropriately to express different value perspectives.

Meaning: Various expressions may be used to make different value statements. Statements may sometimes contain contrasting values.

Procedure: For each of the following statements, have students respond by indicating the two types of value involved.
1. It is the law but I don't like it. _____
2. It is not inexpensive but I don't want it. _____
3. I am expected to do it but I don't like it. _____
4. It is beautiful but not expensive. _____
5. He has chosen a job that is well suited to him; however, the job does not pay well. _____

Value Questions For Discussion
1. What values are in contrast in the above statements?
2. Can you think of other statements that show contrasting values?

Value Dilemma

Have the students discuss the following. A boy is expected to take out the trash, but he hates to do it. What should he do?

Evaluation: Have the students tell about valuing something in two ways.

---

62. A VALUE CHOICE—ETHICAL AND ECONOMIC VALUE

Purpose: To have students become aware of the conflict between ethical value and economic value.

Meaning: The value of the individual may conflict with the value of useful things. The value of the individual is one of infinite meaning and richness, and the value of goods is the usefulness of things.

Procedure: Have students determine what two kinds of value are involved in all the following issues.

Selling a person into slavery.
Child labor.
Forced labor.
Kidnapping a person for ransom.

Value Questions For Discussion

1. How is ethical value being subordinated to economic value in the above situations?
2. Which value is more valuable in these situations—ethical or economic?
3. What does ethical value deal with? What does economic value deal with? Which value has the greatest richness and meaning?

Value Definition

The Value of the Individual: A person is considered an infinity of infinities and therefore has a greater value than infinity. (This principle is given as a moral axiom.)

The teacher may present the following to the students.

If you accept the above principle as valid, what choices would you make in the following situations?

1. Would you free the slaves or not? Give reasons.

2. If you were a factory owner in the 1900's, would you employ child labor or not?
3. If you were a sea captain in the 18th century, would you for profit transport slaves from Africa to America?
4. If you were a manufacturer in the 20th century, would you for profit use chemicals that might destroy the life or health of employees?

Evaluation: Have the students present an ethical argument against slavery.

---

63. THE MORAL SITUATION

Purpose: To have students determine what kinds of value situations fit in the moral or ethical domain.

Meaning: There are many different types of value situations. Only certain types of value situations are eithical or moral situations (those involving potential improvement or impairment of persons or selves). The content of a person's choice determines whether or not it has an ethical character.

Procedure: Ask the students to indicate (Yes, No, or ?) which of the following situations are ethical situations.
1. Hammering a nail into a wall.
2. Driving a nail through a man's hand.
3. A person arrives late for an appointment.
4. A person drives 80 miles an hour on the highway in order not to be late for an appointment.
5. A manufacturer produces vitamin C.
6. A manufacturer produces a chemical that causes disease in rats.
7. A manufacturer makes clothing treated with a chemical that causes disease in rats.
8. Enjoying a gourmet dinner in the midst of starving people.
9. Julia Child creates a French dish on TV.

(Continued)

10. A person "steps on" other persons in his drive to achieve success.
11. A train engineer ignores a stop signal, risking a fatal accident.
12. A control tower operator does not attend to a small blip approaching another blip on the radar screen.

Value Questions For Discussion
1. Which of the described situations have an ethical or moral character? Why?
2. Which ones affect other individuals?
3. Which do not seem to have a moral character? Why not?

Value Situation
Have the students describe how the statement "Let them eat cake," attributed to Marie Antoinette, indicates an ethical situation.

Evaluation: Have the students write about an ethical situation.

---

64. WHICH CHOICES HAVE MORAL SIGNIFICANCE?
Purpose: To have students determine choices that have a moral significance.

Meaning: The content of a person's choice determines whether or not it has a moral significance.

Procedure: Ask students to determine which of the following personal choices have moral or ethical significance.

Whether I travel by plane or car.
Whether I smoke or do not smoke.
Whether I abuse a child.
Whether I care for a sick person.
Choosing a lifestyle.
Favoring a law that would help the poor improve themselves.

Value Questions For Discussion

1. Which choices seem to have a moral or ethical significance? Why?
2. Which choices do not have ethical significance? Why not?

Value Situation

Have the students identify three important ethical choices made by people of the past.

Evaluation: Have the students describe one moral choice they have made.

---

65. VALUE-BLINDNESS

Purpose: To have the students value the meaning of the different value realms.

Meaning: Each value realm has its own significance, which can be identified, clarified, and expressed. The meanings of the various value realms can also be compared and contrasted.

Procedure: Ask students to write responses to the following.

Imagine a person being value-blind in the ways described below. What would the world look like? What would be lost to such a person?

1. To be blind to the value of beauty.
2. To be blind to the value of an individual self.
3. To be blind to the value of social responsibility.
4. To be blind to the value of the law.
5. To be blind to the value of goods and services.

Value Questions For Discussion

1. Tell what the loss might be if a person is blind to economic value, to legal value, to esthetic value, to ethical value, to social value.
2. What is the gain of appreciating economic value, legal value, esthetic value, ethical value, social value?

Value Situations

Have students participate in the following activities.

1. Tell about a person who is considering only one value.
   Examples:
   a. Seeing individuals only as functioning in a role.
   b. Viewing art only in terms of its cost.
   c. Considering a child only from the point of view of satisfying his wants.
2. Scrooge viewed the world only from an economic perspective. Describe his characteristics and describe his value-blindness.

Evaluation: Have the students tell how the world would look to someone viewing it only in a technological way.

Chapter 12

THREE DIMENSIONS OF VALUE:
Intrinsic, Practical, Technical

There are three basic dimensions of value—three critical perspectives from which to value the world. *Intrinsic value* is the value of involvement and unique immediate experience. *Practical value* consists in things valued for their characteristics or descriptive qualities. *Technical value* is the value of synthesis, structure, systematic relationship, and order.

Students can value a given situation in one or more of these dimensions. One can deal with anything intrinsically by involving oneself with it, practically by classifying it, and technically by mental construction and systematization.

Terms such as *involvement, "peak experience," intrinsic, special,* and *unique* indicate intrinsic value; *useful, practical, extrinsic, commonality* indicate practical value; *systematic, formal, structured,* and *relational* indicate technical value.

Valuing from the perspectives of the dimensions gives a hierarchy of richness and meaning, the value of involvement having the greatest richness, the practical values having greater usefulness but less richness, and the technical values having greatest accuracy and precision but less richness and practicality.

This chapter presents activities that will encourage students to view the world from the different perspectives of the value dimensions. The activities will help students to view a given situation from all three perspectives and also to select the value dimension(s) most appropriate to a situation.

66. THREE DIMENSIONS OF VALUE

Purpose: To have the students value a given situation from the points of view of three different value dimensions.

Meaning: Any given situation may be viewed from the different perspectives of the three value dimensions—practical value, technical value, and the value of involvement (intrinsic value).

Procedure: Tell the students that doctors and doctoring will be viewed in three different ways.
   I. Ask the students to *describe* doctoring. Have them list as many specific characteristics and activities of doctors as they can. For example: prescribes medicine, has medical training, diagnoses illnesses, gives medical treatment, etc.
   II. Ask the students to *define* the term "doctor." The definition must give only the *essential* qualities a person *must* have in order to be considered a doctor. Such a definition can be used to determine whether a person *is* a doctor or *not*. For example: "a doctor" could be precisely defined as any person who has a medical degree from an accredited university.
   III. Present the following poem to the students, inviting them to think about how it differs from their description of doctoring and their definition of "doctor."

PHYSICIAN'S PRAYER

Lord, who on earth didst minister
   To those who helpless lay
In pain and weakness, hear me now
   As unto Thee I pray:
Give to mine eyes the power to see
   The hidden source of ill,
Give to my hand the healing touch
   The throb of pain to still,
Grant that my ears be swift to hear
   The cry of those in pain,
Give to my tongue the words that bring
   Comfort and strength again.
Fill thou my heart with tenderness;
And when in weariness I sink,
   Strengthen thou me anew.

Value Questions For Discussion

1. When might it be useful to think about doctoring by considering all the many descriptive characteristics and activities of doctors?

> (To decide whether a particular person is a *good* doctor—whether he or she has all or most of the attributes of our idea of a doctor—either in general or for a given situation.)

2. When might it be necessary to use a formal, precise definition of "doctor"?

> (To find out whether a person is really a doctor or not; or, to find out exactly how many doctors there are in a particular group, community, etc.)

3. How does the person who wrote the poem view doctoring? How does the poem express involvement?

Value Situation

Have the students develop concepts of parenting in each of the three value dimensions.

Evaluation: Have the students represent the activity of being a chef in a practical way (descriptive characteristics), in a technical way (precise definition), and in an intrinsic way (as personally involved).

---

67. ONE SITUATION: THREE VALUE DIMENSIONS

Purpose: To have students view a situation from the points of view of the three value dimensions.

Meaning: The same situation may appear in three value variations. The situation may be valued intrinsically, practically, and technically. Intrinsic value is the value of involvement and immediate experience. Practical value is things valued for their characteristics or descriptive qualities. Technical value is the value of structure, systematic relationship, and order.

Procedure: Have the students read the following selection by Ortega y Gasset.

A great man is dying. His wife is by his bedside. A doctor takes the dying man's pulse. In the background two more persons are discovered: a reporter who is present for professional reasons, and a painter whom mere chance has brought here. Wife, doctor, reporter, and painter witness one and the same event. Nonetheless, this identical event — a man's death — impresses each of them in a different way. So different indeed that the the several aspects have hardly anything in common. What this scene means to the wife who is all grief has so little to do with what it means to the painter who looks on impassively that it seems doubtful whether the two can be said to be present at the same event.[1]

Value Questions For Discussion

1. Who is involved most completely — in an intrinsic way? Tell about the wife's involvement.
2. How does the doctor value the scene professionally and technically? What technical expertise does he bring to bear?
3. For the reporter this is an everyday event. How might he describe the scene in his report?
4. The painter here is concerned with recording or copying the scene on canvas. What are some technical concerns he has regarding his problem of creating a visual image? How might his technical concerns distance him from the event?

Evaluation: Have the students take a flower as an example. Ask them to tell how a botanist might view it technically, how a florist might view it practically, and how a boyfriend/girlfriend might view it intrinsically.

---

68. VALUE PROGRESSION

Purpose: To have students view intrinsic relationships as emerging from practical and/or formal relationships — that values may develop from other values.

Meaning: Intrinsic relationships (except those of the family) grow out of technical and/or practical relations. This takes place through

---

[1]Ortega y Gasset, *The Dehumanization of Art and Notes on the Novel* (Princeton: Princeton Univ. Press, 1948), p. 14.

processes of enrichment. In this process there are distinct leaps from one value dimension to another.

Procedure: Present the following to the students, showing how a tehcnical relationship leads to a practical relationship, which in turn develops into an intrinsic relationship.

Technical relationship : Paying a clerk for a traffic violation.

Practical relationship : Taking the clerk out for dinner.

Intrinsic relationship : Marrying the girl.

Questions For Discussion

1. Which relationship shows the greatest involvement?
2. How did the intrinsic relationship emerge from the technical and extrinsic (practical) relationships?

Value Situation

Have the students tell how an intrinsic relationship with a friend developed from a technical and/or practical relationship.

Evaluation: Have the students show how the intrinsic relationship of trust emerges from technical and/or practical group processes.

---

69. THE VALUE OF INVOLVEMENT AND EXPERIENCE

Purpose: To have students identify instances of the value of involvement and experience.

Meaning: Intrinsic value (the value of involvement and experience) emerges when something fulfills or corresponds to unique or metaphorical concepts. The value of involvement is evoked when things, events, persons are viewed in their singularity.

Procedure: Have students determine which of the following statements express involvement and which do not.

1. What a joyous occasion!
2. He is deeply committed to his work.

(Continued)

3. She gets intrinsic satisfaction from listening to Beethoven.
4. What a magnificent thing!
5. She delights in her cooking.
6. He never enjoys himself.
7. She has no spirit.
8. She marvels at her baby.
9. The artist has lost faith in his work.
10. The explorer was awe-struck.
11. He is indifferent to everything.
12. They have lost the childhood ability of immediate experience.
13. He is not committed to anything.
14. She stands apart from events.

Value Questions For Discussion

1. Which statements indicate the highest degree of involvement?
2. Which statements indicate lack of involvement?
3. Can you describe an intrinsic experience that you or another person has had?

Value Situation

Have the students try to find statements, by persons in real life or literature, that indicate intrinsic involvement.

Evaluation: Have the students select three examples of persons' involvements or experiences and describe and characterize the involvements by statements.

---

70. THE VALUE OF GETTING INVOLVED

Purpose: To have the students become involved with things in an intrinsic way.

Meaning: The highest level of intrinsic value is for one to become deeply involved in experience of the world. There are degrees of involvement, ranging from relatively little involvement to profound and deep involvements. One way to increase involvement is to have persons explore the characteristics of a thing very intensively and continuously over a period of time.

Procedure: Have the students attempt to become involved with the listed items. Ask them to explore the specific characteristics and qualities of each thing until they become more and more involved in it and experience it more and more fully. Tell them to look at each thing in as many different ways and places as they can, and imagine the thing in as many situations and places and times as they can.

a flower	a leaf
a prism	a diamond
perfume	a crystal
a kitten	a jellybean

Value Questions For Discussion

1. How did you become more and more involved in each object?
2. Did you see any of the objects in a new or special way?

Value Situation

Have the students write about something they were very involved with at a particular time in their lives.

Evaluation: Have the students engage in an activity that has the potential of getting them involved (e.g., sports, playing a game, reading a poem). Ask them to express their involvement, verbally or in writing.

---

71. THE VALUE OF UNIQUE ACTIONS

Purpose: To have students determine that actions may fulfill a unique concept.

Meaning: Metaphorical actions condense the qualities of a person's actions and produce a focus or unity.

Procedure: The teacher may have the students read the oath of office of the President of the United States and then discuss it.

Questions For Discussion

1. How does the one action bring together, condense, unify a whole series of discrete separate acts (i.e., as in the Presidential oath)?
2. What are some of the discrete actions a President will take during his term of office that are represented metaphorically, in a unified way, by his taking the oath?

Value Situation

Have the students discuss how marriage vows condense a whole lifetime of separate actions for two people.

Evaluation: Have the students show how peoples' actions are unified or brought together when they pledge allegiance to the flag.

---

72. INDIFFERENCE TO THE VALUE OF INVOLVEMENT

Purpose: To have the students view the world from the perspective of indifference to intrinsic value.

Meaning: Lack of intrinsic value produces indifference to the world. This lack of personal involvement results in cynicism, anomie, and loss of faith and commitment.

Procedure: The teacher may ask students to consider which of the following statements indicate indifference to the value of involvement.

1. Is anything worth while?
2. I care about what happens.
3. I count all my blessings.
4. It all looks the same to me.
5. I have completely lost faith.
6. I treasure my experiences.
7. I couldn't care less.
8. I am a slave to my job.
9. Nothing seems funny to me anymore.
10. Who cares about anything?

Value Questions For Discussion

1. Describe what a person would be like if he or she were indifferent to the world.
2. What is the value of being involved in the world?
3. What is the loss of one who is not involved?

Value Situation

Have the students select and describe literary characters who display indifference to the world.

Evaluation: Have the students list three acts that would indicate indifference to the world.

---

73. UNIQUE VALUE AND THE METAPHOR

Purpose: To have students use metaphors to construct unities and wholes — unique concepts.

Meaning: Metaphors are linguistic representatives of unique ideas. Metaphors condense the disparate or separate characteristics of things and form unities — one quality represents an infinity of other qualities.

Procedure: Have students read the following list and tell how each name brings together many entities, processes, and qualities into one unique image, representing all instances of something.

Cupid	The Red Cross
Neptune	Sir Lancelot
Atlas	Robin Hood
The Great White Whale	The Star Spangled Banner

Value Questions For Discussion

1. How do these metaphors condense broad general experiences and events?
2. What are some of the discrete phenomena that are brought together in the image of Neptune?

Evaluation: Have the students write a metaphor that unifies all the instances or features of something.

74. THE VALUE OF FORMAL DEFINITION

Purpose: To have the students construct formal definitions, thereby creating formal or technical value.

Meaning: Persons can view anything technically by means of a mental construction such as a formal definition or scientific model or formula.

Procedure: Have the students define each of the things listed below as a logical subclass, by constructing a definition. The definition indicates two essential things. It should indicate a *genus*, the larger class to which the subclass belongs, and a *differentia*, which specifies the distinguishing characteristics of the subclass. For example: A rational animal is an animal that has the powers of reason. *Animal* is the genus and *rational* differentiates the subclass of reasoning animals from all other animals.

matriculated student   naturalized citizen
licensed driver   registered Democrat
registered voter   medical doctor

Value Questions For Discussion
1. What do definitions determine about the things defined?
2. Are there instances where things do not conform to your definitions? (E.g., are there such things as *un*licensed drivers?)

Value Situation
Have the students find definitions that have been constructed for the following.
aquanaut and astronaut
electric car
horse

Evaluation: Have the students construct a formal definition for income tax payer.

75. TECHNICAL VALUE

Purpose: To have students value phenomena as formal or logical constructions.

Meaning: Things can be viewed as having technical value. To see a thing technically or formally is to see it in only its definitional or logical qualities. A formal concept is a mental construct—a logical relationship. To see a thing concretely, on the other hand, is to see it in all of its many qualities.

Procedure: Ask the students to find which part of each statement illustrates a thing having purely logical existence and which illustrates a thing having concrete existence.

1. I can see two bananas or two apples, but I cannot see the number two.
2. I am my brother's keeper, not my male sibling's keeper.
3. I do not drink the formula H_2O; I drink water.
4. I feel the pull of gravity, not its formula.
5. I ride my horse, not an *Equus caballus*.
6. I pet my dog and not a *Canis familiaris*.
7. I water my lilac but not a *Syringa vulgaris*.

Value Questions For Discussion

1. What is the difference between viewing things logically or definitionally and viewing them as part of concrete experience?
2. What kinds of names or terms indicate that things can be experienced concretely in the everyday world?

Value Situation

Have the students treat the following logically (definitionally) and also concretely (descriptively).

fog   lake   moon

Evaluation: Have the students tell how a hurricane could be viewed logically (definitionally) and also concretely (descriptively).

76. TECHNICAL NAMES

Purpose: The purpose of this activity is to have students apply technical and scientific value to phenomena.

Meaning: Technical and scientific value is the value of structure, system, and logical relation. Technical names refer to processes that are structured.

Procedure: Have the students read the scientific names listed below (and look up their meanings if necessary). Then ask the students to find more scientific names from the areas of meteorology, aeronautics, medicine, law, chemistry, physics, geology, engineering, astronomy.

Technical and Scientific Names
niacin
fibula
incisors
low pressure system
nebula
fissure
H_2O
$$v = \frac{d}{t}$$

Value Questions For Discussion

1. To what actual things do the technical names refer?
2. What is the relationship that technical names express?

Value Situations

Have the students play the following roles, using scientific language.
doctor and druggist
navigator and ship captain
pilot and copilot
computer programmer and computer
two meteorologists

Evaluation: Have the students list five technical names.

77. CONTRASTING TECHNICAL, PRACTICAL, AND
INTRINSIC VALUE

Purpose: To have the students apply three value dimensions to phenomena.

Meaning: The three value dimensions are characterized by the use of special language — the general language of every day, the more precise language of the technical realms, and the language of unique involvement.

Procedure: Have the students discuss the language terms listed below as indicating the three value dimensions. Then have them add other value expressions to the lists.

Practical Name	Technical Name	Intrinsic Name
pain	pathological symptom	Ouch!
airplane	single-engine aircraft	"Spirit of St. Louis"
brother	male sibling	my brother
horse	Equus caballus	"Black Beauty"

Value Questions For Discussion

1. Which names show things in a unique way—as one-of-a-kind?
2. Which names show things in a formal or structured way?
3. Which names show things as members of familiar general classes?

Value Situation

Have the students think of some unique names of some important historical persons and events (such as "The Little Emperor," "The Great War").

Evaluation: Have the students select an item and give a technical name, a unique name, and a practical name.

78. INDIFFERENCE TO TECHNICAL VALUE (1)

Purpose: To have the students view the world from the perspective of indifference to technical value.

Meaning: Magic, alchemy, shamanism, and the like are ways of viewing the world in a non-technical way. By contrast, the modern sciences of chemistry and astronomy view aspects of the world as structured.

Procedure: Have the students read the following selection.

The ore of gold, as might be expected, grows under the influence of the sun. 'According to the opinions of the Sages, gold is engendered from a sulphur, the clearest possible, and properly rectified and purified in the earth, by the action of the sky, principally of the sun, so that it contains no further humour which might be destroyed or burnt by fire nor any liquid humidity which might be evaporated by fire . . . .' [2]

Value Questions For Discussion

1. Does the statement about the development of gold describe the structural processes by which gold is formed? Is gold really formed by the effect of the sun?
2. How does the statement show lack of significant relationship or lack of technology?

Value Situation

Have the students participate in one or more of the following.

1. In each of the following pairs, which person's work is based on valid relationships? Give specific instances of the lack of valid relationship, system, and structure in each case.
   magician, scientist
   alchemist, chemist
   witch doctor, medical doctor
   astrologer, astronomer

---

[2]Mircea Eliade, *The Forge and the Crucible*, trans. by Stephen Corrin (New York: Harper and Row, 1956), p. 49.

2. Explain the non-technical nature of the following superstitions.
    Walking under a ladder is bad luck.
    Breaking a mirror results in seven years of bad luck.
    A rabbit's foot brings good luck.
    A black cat crossing one's path brings bad luck.
3. Contrast the modern practice of medicine with medicine as it was practiced in the United States in the pre-Civil War era (e.g., before the principle of antisepsis was established).

Evaluation: Have the students list one principle that shows technical value and one that does not.

---

79. INDIFFERENCE TO TECHNICAL VALUE (2)

Purpose: To have the students view the world from the perspective of indifference to technical value.

Meaning: Failure to perceive or appreciate technical value produces technical indifference to the world. The world is not viewed in an orderly, systemic, logical, structured way.

Procedure: Have the students determine which statements indicate lack of technical value or show indifference to technical value.
1. The place runs like a machine.
2. Nothing works right.
3. Everything is coming apart.
4. Laws are meant to be broken.
5. It runs like a clock.
6. There is no logic to it.
7. It is all a matter of luck.
8. The human body is a system.
9. The universe is a vast intricate machine.
10. There is no world order.
11. The mind is a complicated computer.
12. There is no form, no pattern.

Value Questions For Discussion

1. Describe what a person would be like if he or she had no interest in or appreciation for technical value.
2. What is the value of technical value?
3. What is the loss of not having technical value?

Value Situations

Have the students participate in one or more of the following activities.

1. Describe how the world might be if it were lacking order, structure, engineering, laws of physics, and so on.
2. Describe the upside-downness of the world of Alice in Wonderland.
3. Contrast the world of modern science with primitive magic in terms of its lawful, structured nature.
4. Contrast fortune-telling with futurology.

Evaluation: Have the students describe 2 acts that show a total indifference to technical value.

---

80. PRACTICAL VALUE

Purpose: To have students use words and phrases that have a practical value meaning.

Meaning: Practical value is defined as the fulfillment of a class concept. A class concept is characterized by a listing of descriptive properties. When a thing fulfills the properties of its class concept, it is considered a good thing. There are a great many words and phrases that indicate the degree to which a thing fulfills its class concept. *Good, fair, average, poor, no good* are basic practical value terms. There are of course also many linguistic equivalents for such terms: *excellent, fine, OK, so-so, deficient, rotten,* and so on.

Procedure: Have the students indicate which of the following statements or expressions signify that a thing fully fulfills its class concept.

That steak won't do at all.
Do you call that a car?
Some boy!
Honor student.
Not much of a house.
Quite a scholar.
The book has no merit.
Prize bull.
Miserable car!
He is a real showman.
This is a "greasy spoon" restaurant.
That hat really does something for you.
That nurse is not worthy of the name.
That chair is good for all practical purposes.
This pen will serve admirably.
She's an honest-to-goodness teacher.

Value Questions For Discussion

1. What are some words or phrases indicating that a thing exemplifies or fulfills its class concept?
2. What words and phrases indicate that a thing does not exemplify or fulfill its class concept?
3. What are some properties or qualities that a "no good" car might lack?

Value Situation

Have the students use words and phrases which have a practical value meaning to describe

a. the skill of a skier.
b. an auto racer.
c. the performance of a secretary.

Evaluation: Have the students write 3 value statements about things that fulfill or conform to the properties of their class.

81. THE PRACTICAL GOOD (1)

Purpose: To have students identify things which fulfill their class concepts.

Meaning: All of the things in the world that have practical value are things which fulfill their class concepts. There is a range of practical goodness. Terms such as *good, fair, poor, no good,* and their equivalents are used to denote a range of goodness.

Procedure: The teacher may present the following to students and have them name as many things as they can in each category that are considered "good"—that is, the things which fulfill the properties of their concept.

Good buildings
Worthwhile novels
Great Presidents
Good ski areas
Great athletes
Good racehorses
Great cities
Good performers
Great scientists

Value Questions For Discussion

1. Name as many things in the world as you have time to that fulfill their idea—which are considered good.
2. Name as many things in the world as you have time to that do not fulfill their idea—which are not considered good.

Value Situation

Have the students select 10 categories of things and name something for each category that has all or most of the properties of the category and would be considered a good thing.

Evaluation: Have the students name 2 things that fulfill the idea of transportation and two things that do not.

82. THE PRACTICAL GOOD (2)

Purpose: To have students identify instances of things, persons, or groups that fulfill their class concepts. To have students use value statements to denote that which fulfills its class concept.

Meaning: A thing may be valued according to its possession of class properties. Practical value arises from the fulfillment of a class concept. *Good, great, fine, excellent* are terms used to indicate that a thing possesses all the properties of its class concept—is fully what it ought to be.

Procedure: The teacher may have the students construct value statements similar to those listed below which indicate that something fulfills its class concept.
1. Lincoln was worthy to be President.
2. Galileo was what I call a scientist.
3. Pelé is a great athlete.
4. _____ is a fine building.
5. _____ is a great invention.
6. _____ is an excellent performer.

Value Questions For Discussion

1. How does Galileo fulfill the idea of scientist? Does he have all the attributes of a scientist? Does he fully exemplify your idea of scientist?
2. Does Pelé fully exemplify the idea of athlete? In what way?
3. Name some other persons who fully fulfill the idea of scientist, athlete, mayor.

Value Situation

Have the students find examples which fully fulfill or exemplify these concepts.

tennis player
gem
movie
newspaper or TV reporter

Evaluation: Have the students name 4 things that fully fulfill their concepts.

---

83. "BEST" AND "WORST"

Purpose: To have students apply the value predicates "best" and "worst" to persons, objects, and events which are the best in their class and the worst in their class.

Meaning: A thing is the "best" of its kind if it is the one and only member that has the maximum properties of its class. A thing is the "worst" of its kind if it is the one and only member that has the minimum properties of its class.

Procedure: Give the students the following list of items. Have them indicate the class to which each item belongs and then which items are the "best" and which are the "worst" of their class.

The Grand Canyon	"Black Tuesday"
Man-of-War	Thomas Edison
Socrates	Houdini
Ford "Edsel"	Mt. Everest
Titanic	Sherlock Holmes

Value Questions For Discussion

1. Name the class that the Grand Canyon is the "best of."
2. What properties does this class have?
3. What attributes or properties does the Grand Canyon have that make it the "best" in its class?
   (Proceed in the same manner to discuss the other items in the activity.)

Value Situation

Present the students with the following list of persons' names. Each of these persons has been considered by many to be the best in his or her class. Have the students select one or more of them and list some qualities they think made them the best, at least in their time.

Babe Ruth
Walt Disney
Helen Hayes
Enrico Caruso
Charles Lindbergh

Laurence Olivier
Margot Fonteyn
Charles Chaplin
Florence Nightingale

Value Statement

Have the students write an account about an object, event, or person showing it as the "best" in its class. Examples:

a race horse
a musician
an Olympics champion

Evaluation: Have the students give instances of 2 things they consider the best in their class.

---

84. THE "OUGHT" OF PRACTICAL VALUE

Purpose: To have students identify what is needed to have things fulfill their class concepts (be fully what their names imply).

Meaning: "Ought" indicates some quality or attribute that a thing needs in order to fulfill its concept. A thing ought to acquire any class attributes it is lacking, because it is better for a thing to be "good" (fully what it is) than not to be. This is true by implication from the definition of value—a thing is "good" if it fully exemplifies our concept of it.

Procedure: Have the students read statements such as the following and then write similar "ought" statements of their own.

A house ought to have a roof.
Circles ought to be round.
Teachers ought to explain things.
A king ought to have a crown.
Drinking water ought to be clean.
Plants ought to be watered.

(Continued)

Judges ought to be fair.
Clothes ought to fit.
Triangles ought to be three-sided.
A car ought to run.
A person in love ought to be tender.
A nurse on duty ought to stay awake.
Tables ought to have at least three legs.

Value Questions For Discussion

1. Why do we say a house ought to have a roof?
2. What else does the idea of house include?
   (Continue in the same manner to discuss the other "ought" statements.)

Value Situation

Have the students tell why a policeman ought to enforce the law and why a doctor ought to help the sick.

Evaluation: Have the students describe what cities ought to have to fully fulfill the idea of "city."

---

85. INDIFFERENCE TO PRACTICAL VALUE

Purpose: To have the students view the world from the perspective of indifference to the range of extrinsic "goodness."

Meaning: Things can be judged in terms of a range of goodness — from good to fair to no good. Indifference to such degrees of goodness or extrinsic value results in failure to value things fully — to discern and appreciate excellence.

Procedure: Have the students consider these statements and indicate which ones show indifference to extrinsic or practical value.

1. Things are getting better.
2. There is no best way—it is all the same.
3. There is no greatness in the world.

4. There is no sense of excellence.
5. One thing is no better than another.
6. Some things have more value than others.
7. There is goodness in the world.
8. Everything is mediocre.

Value Questions For Discussion

1. How do some statements show failure to recognize different degrees of goodness?
2. What is the loss of not being able to make a distinction between things that are good, fair, bad, no good, better, worse, etc.?

Value Situation

Have the students describe the loss if there were no range of goodness or sense of excellence in the following areas.

music   cooking   painting

Evaluation: Have the students write two statements that indicate indifference to degrees of goodness.

---

86. THE OPTIMIST AND THE PESSIMIST

Purpose: To have the students use optimistic thinking to place things in correspondence with concepts that make them appear good or valuable.

Meaning: Optimistic thinking is applying the proper concept to a thing. The proper concept is the one which fits the thing and contains all the properties of the thing. Optimistic thinking is placing a thing under an appropriate concept and so make the thing good or valuable. It is the art of always finding that concept which makes things appear good. By contrast, the pessimist tends to use concepts that make things appear bad or not valuable.

Procedure: Have the students distinguish between the value optimist and the value pessimist in these descriptions:

1. Looks at an old dress and says it will make a good rag.
2. Looks at a beat-up car and calls it a good jalopy.
3. Looks at a messy room and says, "It looks nice and lived-in."

Value Question For Discussion

How does matching things to different concepts produce different values?

Value Situation

Have the students role-play a value optimist in the following situations.
A snow storm
Being out of work
Being sick

Evaluation: Have the students place the following things with concepts that make them appear good.

        a puddle   mud   wind

Index of Activity Titles